Acts of Love

Ami DeRienzo

DEDICATION

In memory of Jake Jacobsen, one of the most inspiring people that I have ever known. Not a day goes by that I don't think of you and am grateful that God brought you into my life. You encouraged me to pursue my dreams, and this one is for you, my friend. Wish you were still here to tease me about how many words I've used, and how long it took you to muddle through it.

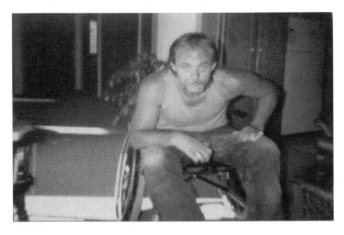

I hope someday the story of this amazing man will find its way to print. At the age of twenty-two, Jake went from being an avid skier and athlete to spending the remainder of his life confined to a wheelchair. Despite his many challenges, Jake served as a mentor to students at the high school in Scarborough, Maine for years, encouraging and inspiring them to never give up and to face whatever battles that may come with courage, hope, and determination. He was passionate about the people and things he loved, and he truly loved "his kids" as he referred to the hundreds of students he mentored. Jake had a unique ability to put life in perspective for those around him through his gift of pointing out that which is trivial and not worth making a fuss about. Jake died peacefully in his sleep on October 14, 2016 at the age of sixty-five, after his part in making the world a better place was complete.

ACKNOWLEDGMENTS

To my partner Katy for standing by my side for the past fifteen years and teaching me what it is like to finally experience "normal"

To my family for your love and support

To my therapist Dr. White for getting me through my darkest times with your kind and compassionate ways

To the many teachers and staff at Shaw Junior High and Gorham High School

To all those who helped make this project possible through their generous sponsorship including Neil Foley, Sharon Picard, Steve Brydon, Kate St.Clair, Sally Rogers, Maureen Burns, my parents, my brothers David & John, and so many others...

To each and every one of you who were a part of my journey along the way... For every kind word, for every smile, for every day that you chose love... Thank you...

Ami DeRienzo

INTRODUCTION

Some little girls grow up dreaming they will become a rock star or a princess. That wasn't me. One thing I knew for sure was that I wanted to live with Ma and Pa Ingalls on the Prairie where I would catch frogs and stand proudly by Laura's side while she took on Nellie. I wanted to experience how that potato would feel on my tongue with salt and no butter, the thrill of licking a sugar cube, and the sting of the ice pellets on my face while trying to find my way to the barn during the Big Winter. Being from Maine, one would think the latter might not have held quite so much appeal, but the idea of someone being unable to see the hand in front of their face sounded like a pretty amazing experience to me, at least the way Laura told it.

When I wasn't dreaming about living life in the 1800s, I was fantasizing about running away with my best friend and becoming a daddy to her children. I don't think the word transgender even existed back then, and if it did, I wouldn't have known it. What I did know, however, was that I loved that girl and nothing would have made me happier than to spend forever with her, preferably running through fields and hanging out with Laura. There was nothing political or sexual about it. I just knew girls were supposed to marry boys who would inevitably take them away from their friends and family. The only way to spend my life with the girl I loved was obviously to be a boy. It was the logical solution to what at the time didn't seem like a terribly complicated issue. I was also far too young to consider that there might be options that were not on my radar back when the world was simple.

Though my childhood love eventually moved away and other things didn't turn out quite the way I'd planned, that sense of wonder and longing to experience things to their fullest was never completely extinguished. Like many kids who one day are confronted with the harshness of reality, I discovered that Laura Ingalls was dead and that life in the 1800s likely wasn't anywhere near as fun as she made it sound. I learned to accept the fact that I was indeed a girl and that it was physically impossible for me to ever be someone's daddy. I also found that potatoes without butter are really not at all exciting but that a good writer can make even ordinary things sound incredible. Despite these brutal awakenings, I survived the disappointment and continued to dream. Maybe my dreams became a little more conservative, my love a bit more guarded, and my quest for adventure more risk-averse, but inside I never stopped wanting to live my life the way Laura did, savoring the magic of everyday experiences, loving in the moment, and taking nothing for granted along the way.

There was a time in my life when my sanity was questioned, and when the probability of ever achieving the status of adulthood was deemed unlikely at best. I don't remember exactly when it all began, but I do remember the first time I took a kitchen steak knife and drove it into my flesh when I was just eleven years old. I remember the first time I tried to end my life in the sixth grade by downing a bottle of aspirin and the overwhelming urges I had to self-destruct in the years that followed. I remember feeling like I needed to break through the numbness that had taken hold and was preventing me from experiencing the sense of wonder I once knew, that perhaps the knife could cut through the shroud of darkness that encased me and could somehow set me free. I remember feeling trapped in my own body, a body I grew to hate more and more every day as nature took its course, thrusting me into a world of feminine hygiene and icky girl parts. I remember wanting to go back, to be the kid who found joy in building forts and pretending to be someone I wasn't, wishing that I could find pleasure again in the simple things and escape to a world where it was possible to believe in dreams coming true.

I don't know if it was the onslaught of puberty or any one of a number of reasons that caused this time from preadolescence to adulthood to be so dark. There were issues of sexual identity and mental illness that when combined with normal experiences and hormones I'm sure were contributing factors. Whatever the ultimate cause or trigger, I was a child who wanted to die and who held little hope for the future. In an effort to cope, I did the only thing that seemed to offer any relief which was to withdraw into a world of ritual self-destruction and abuse.

While my darkness seemed to pique at the young age of eleven, as I reflect back and especially when I look at my own nieces and nephews who are around that age, I can appreciate the fact now that I was young. Though I certainly didn't feel like a little girl at the time, in hindsight I am able to see myself through a different lens, and it is hard to imagine a child that age being in such a dark place. Sadly, I know there are many kids who are facing the same darkness, struggling to find their identity and purpose in life. I was blessed to have people who loved me and who never gave up, but having been in that place, I know that sometimes you can be surrounded by love and not recognize it, causing you to feel completely alone. Knowing this to be true, it breaks my heart when I come across young people who are unable to see their own value and how much they are loved.

There are a number of reasons why I chose to share my story in this way. The biggest reason is because I know that there are young people out there who are battling the same demons that haunted me throughout my life and who may feel that they are alone in their darkness. I write because I know that there are also parents of children who have no idea what to do or how to reach their little ones who are crying out for help. While I don't pretend to have the answers, one thing God has blessed me with is experience. In the pages that follow, I will share some of these experiences with you with the hope that there may be something here to which you can relate or perhaps make you feel a little less alone. Thank you for sharing this journey with me as I venture back into the darkness.

Ami DeRienzo

CHAPTER 1

The older I get, the more I find myself living life with a sense of foreboding, wondering if today will be the day when I get the call that something dreadful has happened to someone I love or that the result of what is normally a routine physical now suddenly carries a death sentence. Having been blessed in so many ways, when I see those around me suffering, it makes me wonder when my turn is going to come. I know carrying this fear is no way to live, and while I do try not to dwell on what could happen and focus on enjoying the life that I have been given, sometimes it is hard to shake that feeling of impending doom.

Because of my past, I often feel like I am living on borrowed time, that eventually it is all going to catch up with me. My hope is that when it does, it will come before I have to experience anything that for me would be worse than death like losing a sibling, niece, nephew, or partner. While losing one of my parents is obviously something that I also dread, I guess I have resigned myself to the inevitability that someday it will happen, and statistically speaking, I will more likely than not be around when it does. In this regard, there is no ideal solution as I know it would hurt just as much to envision them grieving a child as it would for me to grieve one of them. Thankfully, having never had children of my own, I will never live with the constant fear that must come with being a parent. I don't know if my mind or my heart could take it as losing a child has to be the most unimaginable pain one could ever experience.

Another fear that I carry is that someday I will be one of those people who does something incredibly stupid like distracted driving which in turn results in a horrific accident or trauma that can never be taken back. I think of the father who runs over his child playing in the driveway, the person who glances down at their phone or fiddles with the radio for a split second, or the mom who makes that horrible in the moment decision to leave the baby in the car not wanting to wake them up. A split second, a momentary lapse in judgment, and your life is essentially over. Not only is your punishment the internal hell that comes from the guilt and sadness that you will inevitably feel if you are remotely human, but couple that with whatever society deems appropriate in terms of punishment and then add social media, and every meaningful thing you may have ever done in your life up until that moment in time is no longer of any consequence. While I imagine some people learn to survive and somehow move forward at least on the surface, I don't understand how, and fear that I would not have the strength or the will to do so if such a thing were to ever occur, even if it wasn't my fault.

I share these fears with you because throughout my entire life there have been things that I've wanted to do, but it seems the timing for getting those items on my to do list done inevitably fell into the category of some elusive someday. When I was younger, there didn't seem to be any sense of urgency. I would either think of someday as always being there as an option, or I would be in such a depressed state that I didn't care if someday ever came. I wasn't worrying about getting a terminal disease or suddenly realizing that I can't remember what happened five minutes ago. I didn't fear becoming an emotional or mental cripple who couldn't will themselves to get out of bed and face another day due to guilt or grief. If I was going to live, I always thought the things I dreamed about doing would be an option at some point, and in the meantime, I would spend my life doing the things I was supposed to do. The older I get and the more loss and unexpected tragedy I see befall others in my life, the more I am struck with the reality that the someday I have taken for granted my entire life could disappear at any moment without warning.

While I have no inside knowledge of anything particularly horrible about to befall me, it is the fear that it will come unexpectedly that keeps me up at night and compels me to write. It is not so much the fear of my own personal demise through death or physical incapacitation, but rather the fear that a major tragedy could cripple me mentally and emotionally in a way that I am not prepared for and that could send me spiraling back into a world I escaped from so long ago. It is this fear that convinces me that I can no longer wait for that elusive someday. There are a number of things that motivate me to write, but this is certainly one of them, the knowledge that today could be the last someday that I have to share myself in this way with the people that I love.

We all have our own stories, and I'm not so crazy as to think that mine is somehow special. There are millions who have experienced far more in their lifetime than I could ever imagine. Making a lot of bad choices and being diagnosed with a mental illness doesn't make me uniquely qualified to write a book or mean that I necessarily have something that will be of interest to the world. In fact, there are all kinds of people in my immediate circle whose stories are far more traumatic, inspiring, and compelling than mine could ever be. I feel the need to express this because when I write about myself, it makes me feel like a narcissist. I immediately go to that place in my head where I am wondering what you are thinking of me, asking myself if I come across as overindulgent or self-absorbed, melodramatic or just tiresome. My mind gets stuck in a constant state of over-thinking, and I feel the need to explain myself because I'm not special, not the kind of special someone writes a book about anyway.

While we are on the subject of me trying to explain myself to you, I guess it would be appropriate to warn you about how my brain works so that you are prepared for the wind tunnel feeling you may experience as I take you back with me through my memories. First, I must warn you that it will be told through the lens of my current crazy which consists of an aging mind plagued with memory loss and the attention span of a toddler. Many are familiar with the analogy of a dog that sees a squirrel. This is perhaps the best way in which I can describe my mind, as my life is a constant loop of one squirrel moment after another. While I can sit and play with that silly squeeze toy for quite some time (especially if it is located in a casino and comes equipped with multi-lines and bonuses), if you put an activity in front of me that requires sitting still, the universe is suddenly filled with

13

distractions. I ask that you please forgive me for the scattered way in which this story may unfold. My mind races and rambles and pontificates and sometimes stalls as I can't always find the words to communicate effectively and succinctly. For this reason, I will never be a Twitter kind of girl, something my brothers and my buddy Jake used to love to tease me about.

I also realize that some folks can get creeped out when people reveal too much about themselves, sharing secrets that society tells us should be locked away in a closet somewhere. While the world is certainly evolving, many of us come from that old school way of thinking that tells us it is wrong to air our dirty laundry and shameful to admit that we have problems that others don't see. We are taught to speak in hushed tones about things such as mental illness, sexuality, family issues, or the heartache that accompanies grief. Because of this, I will apologize in advance if I make you feel uncomfortable. I do this not because I am some grand exhibitionist, but because I believe that many of us share the same kind of secrets. I also think that when we all walk around pretending our fears don't exist that we ultimately end up with a world full of people who feel completely alone in their pain, not realizing that everyone else is hiding secrets too. For me, this is about speaking to those hurting individuals directly and saying that you are not alone. While our stories may be different, what we all share is a humanity that causes us to experience shame, heartache, and loss, things that make us doubt our own worth and cause us to search desperately for a place where we belong. I have come to believe that it doesn't matter if you are the captain of the football team or the kid getting bullied and shoved into a locker. We are all battling our own demons, and I feel as if it is time to stop being ashamed of the fact that each and every one of us, buried somewhere beneath our masks, is a child who was hurt somewhere along the way.

As I begin this quest of sharing my story, determining where to start is the first major challenge. Despite the chaos that can go on in my head, I am actually quite analytical by nature. I seek order and clarity, a logical and practical means of getting the job done. This analytical side of me would insist I tell my story chronologically from start to finish with a clear beginning and definitive end. There is another me, however, the crazy and chaotic me that rejects any such thing and thinks I should just share the dramatic moments and leave out the rest. Then there is the try to be accommodating me who suggests I should include equal parts of order and disorder. In the end, I think the "wing it" me is about to take over, however, and let it come out naturally however it flows, putting the control freak in me back in my box.

This is part of my problem... Nothing is ever as simple as doing it. Every decision, even something that should be easy like what's for dinner, becomes a war between the many personalities in my head. Crazy me always votes for "Wild West Wednesday" at *Texas Roadhouse,* while the frugal hoarder wants to use up the food surplus I bought on sale three years ago that still sits in the freezer. Meanwhile, my caretaker feels the need to present my partner with a choice between five different meal combinations to make sure she is happy and cared for. Then the indifferent me wants to skip dinner altogether and eat chocolate and ramen while sitting at my desk doing paperwork. Every night it is the same ordeal, mentally exploring all the pros and cons of each option as ambiguous me concludes that all options are plausible and that there is no right or wrong answer. It's never just "I'm hungry. I think I'll make chicken." Not in my world... So I welcome you to my world, and I thank you in advance for your patience.

Before you get the wrong idea... Despite my many characteristics, I am not one of those multiple personality folks. My personalities all co-exist as one unit without their own wardrobes and dialect like you might see on television. Each personality is actually a part of the whole and not separate entities. My many conflicting personality traits fight in the same way I used to fight with my siblings, making it so that I am not very expedient when it comes to decision making. Because of this, to get us moving in the right direction or any direction for that matter, I will begin by sharing with you what I remember from my earliest years in order to appease whatever me it is that is telling me to do it before I go off on another squirrel chasing adventure. Please don't give up on me quite yet, as we have only just begun.

Ami DeRienzo

Journal Entry – June 18, 1991

Today I am a funny face
Emotions set, a smile in place
Laugh my way through all the pain
Until I find myself again

Today I am a rebel child
A reckless heart that's running wild
Partying my life away
Until there comes another day

Today I am a grieving soul
The one who weeps for dreams grown old
Sadly looking to the past
Yet this face soon too will pass

Today I am as hard as steel
Incapable of being real
Brace my nerves, a heart of stone
Today content to walk alone

Today I am a caring sort
Who feels for others when they hurt
Compassion rules this heart of mine
Until there comes another time

Today I am a heart of rage
A lion pacing in a cage
One that I cannot release
And yet another part of me

Today I am a little girl
Scared, alone, and so confused
Wondering who I really am
Tomorrow I'll devise a plan

Ami (6), Beth (8), Matt (4), Sandy (2)

I was never very happy in a dress...

CHAPTER 2

As many kids who have come before me, I grew up with two parents who provided a roof over my head, food on the table, and the foundation of a strong work ethic and moral compass that came in handy later in life. When I entered this world, my parents were in their early twenties and had moved to Maine from their home state of Massachusetts. Thinking back on the person I was when I was in my twenties, it is hard to imagine anyone having the ability to parent successfully at that young of an age, but of course millions of people do it and my parents were no different. My father was a young person fresh out of college, dealing with the knowledge that an injury would prevent him from ever playing professional sports as he had dreamed. My mother had dropped out of college to get married when she met my father and had also given up on a dream to join the Peace Corps. My sister Beth came first, and I followed two years later, the second of what would eventually become a brood of seven children being raised during a span of three decades beginning in the early seventies. Each of us were two years apart with a twelve year age difference between the oldest and the youngest.

When my folks were starting out, they were given an incredible opportunity to purchase a beautiful home that my dad's father had built in the town of Scarborough, Maine. Like many kids from that generation, at a time when hard work and self-sufficiency were considered critical attributes, they decided they wanted to make it on their own and refused help from my grandparents. Instead of purchasing my grandfather's home in an up and coming neighborhood for the miniscule price of $25,000 (now worth close to $500,000), they bought a mobile home in a trailer park in Saco and did it their way. It is just a wild guess, but I'm thinking that may be where I get my independent streak and my ability to be content in humble surroundings. I think I would choose a shack in the woods over an oceanfront mansion, perhaps not every day but on most days. This simple decision, however, also strikes me so many years later as to how our choices in life set off a chain of events that inevitably dictate our fate, like the "Choose Your Own Adventure" books I remember reading as a child. My parents went with option #2 which took them to page thirty-five instead of page sixty-three.

Ironically enough, the home my parents turned down was almost across the street from Jake, the man to whom this book is dedicated, and someone whose path would cross mine about forty years after my parents made the decision not to be his new neighbor. That is one thing I truly love about Maine and its small world connections. It is also something that I love about life, and the incredible way in which people who are meant to be in your life will get there one way or another, even if it takes them forty years. I have found that things have a way of coming together, and while looking at a single group of puzzle pieces or a section of an embroidery project may make no sense at all, when the puzzle or canvas is complete, that which once seemed random suddenly takes on a life of its own and has the potential to become something incredibly beautiful.

My life began in a trailer park as a result of that puzzle piece decision my parents made over forty years ago. My mom stayed home to care for my sister and I, and my dad taught fourth graders during the day and worked a second job at night in the bakery at a local grocery store. As a child, I enjoyed the feeling of community that the park provided us. Things were quite different back in the 70s. Mom would let us out to play and wander around the neighborhood for hours without ever worrying about things like child molesters and kidnappers. While I'm sure they still existed back then, it was not a world of twenty-four seven information overload, so we didn't worry quite so much about all the things that could go wrong or threaten our existence. Every afternoon I would make the rounds and visit my trailer park friends, the old man next door who would invite me in for a can of soda, and the woman across the street who gave me cookies. I was between three and four years old at the time.

One day Mom got a call from a concerned neighbor alerting her to the fact that I was going around asking people for food. Likely embarrassed, my mother reprimanded me for my lack of manners and made me vow never to ask for food again. Being the creative thinker that I was, the next day I went back, only this time instead of asking for food I would scope out the home and if there was fruit in sight, I would say "I like bananas…." If there was a fresh batch of cookies on the counter, my banana line would become "I like cookies…" If they didn't get the hint the first time, I would try again with "I really like bananas…" and if they still didn't get it, I'd keep placing more emphasis on the word "REALLY" until I ultimately got what I came for without having to break the rules and ask for it.

My mom used to laugh and say that I could "talk a starving dog off a meat truck." Guess perhaps I missed my calling in life and probably should have gone to law school or maybe into politics if her assessment was correct. What is interesting to me now as an adult, though, is how quickly at the young age of three I had learned how to get my needs met and adapt to the situation. It also makes me wonder if this is when I learned that it was wrong to clearly state your desires or intentions and instead mastered the art of passive-aggressiveness. I accepted that there was shame in telling people you were hungry or asking directly for something you may want or need. I also found creative ways to fill the voids in my life and gain control in situations when others threatened to take that control away.

We moved out of the trailer park and into a small house in Portland when Mom became pregnant with my little sister Sandy. At the time Beth was six, Matt was almost two, and I was four. As sad as I was to say goodbye to my friends at the park, I was excited to move into our new home, especially upon discovery of the secret passageways that ran through the walls and connected our bedrooms upstairs. The back yard contained the most fabulous weeping willow tree on the planet, perfect for climbing and fort building, despite the fact that it made an awful mess of the yard and threatened to destroy our grouchy neighbor's in-ground pool with its powerful roots.

As I had done in the trailer park, I quickly adapted to my new surroundings, and it didn't take long before I made the acquaintance of my neighbors including the two elderly sisters who lived next door, the kind lady across the street, and the family with the Siamese cat who lived in the house behind us. I was a social creature back then, and loved the attention and coddling I received from people outside the family. My mom tells me that as soon as I became old enough to speak, I started to approach strangers in restaurants asking them if I could go home with them and be their little girl. Apparently with my typical Leo personality, I was not good at sharing the spotlight with my siblings, even as a toddler.

It was at this house in Portland that I discovered my entrepreneurial spirit. My first business venture involved making crosses out of two toothpicks, a piece of Scotch tape, and a great deal of charm. I would take my masterpieces door to door, selling them for twenty-five cents each which was actually a lot of money back then, especially for the goods I was selling. Over the years, my craftsmanship blossomed when my grandmother gave me my first latch-hook kit for Christmas. At this stage, my customers got a little better return on their investment, though I was careful to raise my price points given the added labor and material costs.

My poor neighbors, both at the trailer park and in our new home in Portland, didn't seem capable of saying no to a child who more often than not looked like she had just crawled out of the gutter and appeared to be starving to death with her skeletal frame. It didn't matter how clean I may have been when I left the house or how much my mother may have tried, within minutes of going outdoors I would be covered in filth. It was funny, because my sister Beth was just the opposite. Somehow she could manage to eat an ice cream sundae or even tacos and not have a drop to show for it. Not me... I would come out of the experience looking much like the food I had attempted to eat. Perhaps a more accurate description would be that I looked like the food I was trying to eat after it had been put in a blender. I could also eat all day long and not gain an ounce of fat. The latter was a problem that miraculously corrected itself once I turned forty, much to my dismay. As for the issue of my sloppiness, I've come to accept that I will likely never be cured which is why I have spent most of my adult life wearing black.

Later in life when I was starting out in my career, a store manager pulled me aside one day and told me that I looked like I'd just rolled out of bed, and that he was going to take me on as his next "my fair lady" project, teaching me how to walk and dress like a professional. In the store manager's office, he placed a book on my head and encouraged me to walk back and forth trying to work on my posture. Given the staples in lieu of a hem in my suit pants years later, and the current holes in my sneakers, I don't think he can claim complete success in his attempt at an extreme makeover. In fact, there is a good chance I may be a hopeless cause, at least with regard to fashion, given that some of these attributes seem to have been ingrained in me since early childhood.

Living in Portland resulted in the birth of two more little DeRienzos, Sandy and John. By the time I was eight, we moved once again. This time it was to the town of Gorham. Mom was pregnant with her sixth (David) to be followed by the grand finale, little Joey. The new house was much bigger than anything we'd experienced before, and I quickly grew to love the country life. Unlike Portland where I had a small radius in which I was allowed to explore, Gorham held all kinds of possibilities. This was also the place where the darkness started to become noticeable as I transitioned from cute and innocent looking waif to an isolated and angry preadolescent.

Ami (Age 4) "I like bananas..."

Back: John (6), Sandy (8), David (4)
Front: Matt (10), Beth (14), Ami (12), Joe (2)

CHAPTER 3

We were a diverse bunch of kids, each with our own unique personalities and role to play in the family dynamics. Given the age differences between the oldest and the youngest, the little ones were still quite small when my sister Beth and I both moved out of the house when we turned eighteen. Because of this, it feels like we lost out on experiencing a good portion of our youngest siblings' childhoods. The memories I do have of them, however, are fond ones, mixed with the occasional twinge of guilt for not being the big sister that I could have been had I not been caught up in my own issues. My two youngest brothers were still toddlers when I first began my descent into the darkness, and little Joey was only eight years old on the day I left home and essentially disappeared from their lives for many years.

As our family grew faster than we could keep up with, not only did our dynamics shift, but our ability to do things as a family also changed. Activities like going out to eat or venturing off on a family outing were never easy, and despite my poor memory, I have a good recollection of almost every family outing, because they were special and rather infrequent. Beth and I were able to experience more in our early years than the other kids ever did simply due to the fact that it is much easier to do anything with a few children than it is with seven.

It's funny the memories that stick with you from childhood, stuff that to an adult may seem irrelevant, but can be so significant when you're a kid. I remember how exciting it was to go to *Bonanza* and be able to get my own soda from the soda fountain, to push the ice dispenser lever and watch how the machine magically created ice. People didn't have refrigerators at home back then that made water and could spit out ice cubes (at least no one that I knew), so this was a bit of a novelty. I also remember marveling at how much better the machine root beer tasted compared to the homemade root beer my mom tried to make on special occasions with the powdered root beer packets. For some reason, homemade root beer reminded me all too much of the dreaded powdered milk we used to drink. While powdered root beer was undoubtedly a thousand times better than milk, it was still not the same as the root beer they made at *Bonanza*.

As fondly as I remember our family outings, I don't think I have a single memory that didn't end with at least one of us getting into a heap of trouble and my father vowing that he was never going to take us anywhere ever again. Eventually he would cave, however, only to repeat the vicious cycle when we would try again. As for who the troublemakers in the family were, I would have to say (and I'm sure Mom would agree), John and I were generally the most challenging of the bunch. We were stubborn and independent, not willing to back down from a fight nor were we able to suppress our passions. David, on the other hand, was a different kind of trouble. While John and I were known to act out in anger and defiance fueled by the things we cared about most, David was a prankster, the adorable, goofy kid that made people laugh. Despite his easy going nature and fun loving ways, he also seemed to get in trouble incessantly, getting dragged into a fight with one of his older brothers or teasing little Joey. He had the kind of personality where he liked to get people going, in a playful, antagonistic kind of way.

Beth never got into trouble and was by all accounts a perfect child, and Matt's rebellion didn't really kick in until his teen years. If anything, Matt was the victim of his sometimes cruel older sisters who could be terribly bossy and overbearing at times, especially during those years in which he was the only boy. Sandy was quiet, fun loving, and easy going, taking in everything around her, and typically getting along with everyone just fine, offering a sense of calm and tranquility. Then there was Joey, sweet and gentle Joe who endured getting beat on by his big brothers and yet maintained a spirit of kindness and compassion. Joe was the kind of kid who by the age of six was worrying about children going hungry in Africa and expressing concern for the safety of pole workers having to be out in a storm. He would pick flowers for my mom, or say sweet things that would make you want to scoop him up and give him a hug for being so ridiculously cute.

As a big sister, one of my favorite things to do was to make dinner for the kids. There were times when I would create menus and allow each of my siblings to choose what they wanted for dinner. Mind you, it was nothing fancy with entrees that consisted of things like cereal, blueberry pancakes, and macaroni and cheese, but more often than not I would have seven different meal choices going on for a single dinner. It always made me happy to feel like I could spoil them even for a minute, even if it was only one night of saving them from Mrs. Johnson's casserole or one of my mom's occasional meatloaf experiments. It was so hard to leave the kids behind when I left home that day, as I had dreamt that someday I would take them with me. They were too young to understand all that was going on, and why their big sister suddenly disappeared.

For as long as they could afford it, my parents sent us to a private Christian school where we enjoyed tiny class sizes that often consisted of less than ten kids. While I don't remember much about school other than a traumatic solo I did in the first grade of "Go Tell It On The Mountain," and a few other equally embarrassing in hindsight moments, I remember fondly our trip to *Len Libby's* candy store which back then might as well have been Willy Wonka's factory. There were also the annual field trips to the *Fryberg Fair* which would inevitably be a disappointment being that we didn't have money for rides or cotton candy. I liked animals and all, but being a kid and watching other kids have fun is not cool, especially at the fair. And who could forget the yearly magazine and book sale drives... To this day I still have an appreciation for anyone who buys *The Reader's Digest* as this magazine always came with the coolest of prizes.

As for other memories during those early years, I remember the trips to *Kmart* and how excited the grownups would get when that blue light special was announced, and the time my sister Beth and I got to sit at the food counter and share an ice cream. I also remember thinking that the *Maine Mall* was a great place for an adventure, particularly around the holidays when they would have it decked out with creative Christmas displays and live nativity scenes. No reward ever meant quite so much as that third place cow milking ribbon I received at the mall one year. There were only three of us, but I got my very own ribbon and to me that was special. Perhaps this is where the "everyone gets a trophy" philosophy originated, and if I was in any way representative of a typical kid, I can see why they would think it would be a wildly successful endeavor. Despite my admiration of the cow and love for my ribbon, however, the baby goats were my favorite, and after they ate all the buttons from my button down shirt, I decided someday I would have a baby goat all of my own. That is one item still on the bucket list, way down there at the bottom after I get my chimpanzee and my orangutan.

The things we remember... Looking back, I don't remember what toys I got for Christmas or what the silly fights were about that I had with my siblings and parents over the years. What I do remember are the times when I felt special and the times when I wanted to die. And then all those random, silly things in between like Mom's soybean pancakes that I expected would be horrible but were surprisingly good, and that day she made homemade peanut butter playdough which we all loved playing with almost as much as we did eating it.

With regard to grammar school, I remember being one of the last kids to get picked for the team in gym class and not having someone to share lunch with in first grade. I remember getting in fights on the playground and hanging out with the teacher, because I didn't have many friends. Permanently chiseled into my memory is that mean girl who dug her fingernails into my arm so deep as to leave indentations and draw blood, and I can still feel those bird like talons that had me in their vice. There are memories of riding on the school bus, and the eraser bit collection I shared with my friend whose mom used to take her teeth out and brush them in front of us.

I remember the high school girl named Bridget who took a moment one day to tell me she thought I was a pretty cool kid, a memory I held on to and cherished throughout my life. Many years later when I heard that she killed herself, it made me wonder if she saw my sadness even back then and if that is why she took the time to tell a little kid that they were special. I wonder if she saw herself in me, that lost tomboy who didn't quite fit in. Hearing of her death made me wish that I had found her later in life and told her how much her simple comment that day meant to me, how she had inspired and given hope to a kid who thought she was cool too. I wish I had the chance to tell her how important and how loved she was before that horrible day when she decided that life was no longer worth living. I wish we could have walked through our darkness together, and perhaps she too could have found another way.

Ami DeRienzo

Journal Entry – August 16, 1989

If only I could have talked with her. It should have been ME in that coffin, not Bridget. She shouldn't have been alone. If I'd known what she was going to do, I'd have been there with her and done it too, if I had to. How could she leave me here like this? I wonder if she even remembered me at all. It's funny how someone can touch so many lives and not even know it. I'm sure she never knew how much I loved her.

I went to the cemetery and said goodbye. I got down on my knees and cried and talked and cried some more. Two old ladies stopped by while I was there. They came over and looked at the flowers, trying to decide what kind they were and whether this one was "real or fake." I felt like screaming. Before they left, they said, "What a shame, only 22 years old..." I bought a rose and put it with the rest of the flowers. I wish I could have just stayed there all night with my head on the ground.

Ami DeRienzo

CHAPTER 4

Life was full of rituals back when we were kids. In the morning Dad would stand in the kitchen and give my mom a kiss before heading off to work, and there was bound to be at least one disgusted "Ewe..." More often than not, it would be coming from me. We would then do the things that kids do until it got to be mid-morning which is when we would line up to get our snack. We had 10 o'clock and 2 o'clock snacks every day, and the time in between seemed like an eternity.

As the afternoon would begin to wind down, we'd anxiously await my father's return from school, greeting him with enthusiastic screams of "Daddy's home!!!!" Most days we were happy to see him. In fact, when I had a black lab later in life who would greet me at the door with a shoe, I would think back on these days when I would wait for my father to come home. The only times we weren't excited to see him was when something had happened during the day to warrant delayed punishment. Though my mom was typically the disciplinarian in the house, if we were particularly horrid she would pull him into the mix, a role he hated to play especially after a long day at work.

On these days, I would dread hearing the slam of the car door. "Just wait until your father gets home..." was not something we ever wanted to hear on a day when we had been behaviorally challenged. This too was an instance in which more often than not I was the guilty party. Being the creative and practical thinker that I was, I remember putting books down my pants to try to create some extra padding. There was nothing quite like being told that the punishment for something you did was not going to come until several hours later. Makes me wonder if death row inmates endure this same kind of agony... Being that my father was so seldom involved in the disciplinary process, it was also a fear of the unknown. In the end, the punishment never ended up being anywhere near as bad as the fear and anticipation that led up to it. Typically, discipline was immediate and swift, but when it wasn't, you knew you were in for an afternoon of mental torture wondering what that punishment was going to look like.

On most days, my dad would come in and be immediately overwhelmed by his brood of hellions. My mom would grab her purse, ready to make the great escape to *Burger King* for a long and quiet cup of coffee. This was a part of the ritual where my frazzled mother who had spent the day dealing with our antics would have an hour or two to escape. My sister would take charge, and the battles would begin. As I mentioned earlier on, it was a different world back then, and my sister was only about nine when she started babysitting for us. By the age of twelve, she was playing Mom to all six of her younger siblings.

Beth was not a typical child and was far more like a miniature sized adult. I guess being the eldest of that many kids would indeed make someone age prematurely. She could cook, clean, do laundry, and manage to carry a baby at the same time. Though she had many skills, she was still my sister, and there were times when I didn't always respect the chain of command when she was left in charge. It was one thing to be told to clean my room by my mother, but having my nine year old sister telling me what to do was another thing entirely. Of course if you ever saw the condition of my room, you would know that I didn't listen to either of them very well.

Though most of her babysitting adventures were not this exciting, I remember one day I got in all kinds of trouble for pulling a butcher knife on my sister and threatening to kill her. When my parents got home, I had a lot of explaining to do. The defense I attempted to use was that she was going to smash me over the head with a chair, but they would have none of it. My sister's side of the story was that the chair was simply a means of protecting herself from her psychotic little sister's knife. I'm guessing I must have been around six or seven at the time. Ironic how one of my few memories of getting in all kinds of trouble as a kid had to do with a knife and the other had to do with food. Maybe it was an omen of what was to come...

Most days were not quite so dramatic. My dad would get home from teaching and take my mom out for their daily coffee rendezvous. We would have dinner which typically consisted of pasta, pasta, or more pasta with an occasional chicken or maybe Shepard's pie if it was a special day or if Dad had gotten another loan from the credit union. This was definitely one of our all-time favorites. At each meal, we would eat like we hadn't been fed in weeks, and my dad would hover off in the corner, making sure we got what we needed before he would fill his plate. If there was enough left over for seconds, it would inevitably go to one of the children. Though I never appreciated it then or even realized the selflessness behind their daily sacrifices, as an adult I can reflect back on these little things that now take on such deeper meaning.

Sometimes my dad couldn't be home for dinner, depending on what time his second shift job would start. On these nights, he would come home and change from his suit and tie into his grocery store uniform and head off to the bakery. As much as we hated that he was never around, we all loved that he worked at the grocery store. In those days, things were different. Companies were not afraid of lawsuits and liabilities. Employees were family who took care of each other, and the world wasn't quite so uptight. Back then my dad was allowed to bring home the bakery trash that they normally would donate to the pig farms, the day old breads and sweets that could no longer be sold but were perfectly good to eat. There was no excitement like when we looked out the window and saw Dad carrying two giant trash bags from the bakery. It was like Christmas, and the thrill of busting into those bags never got old.

You would think he had brought home a piñata. He would command us all to back away and would place his catch in the middle of the room for the big reveal. Then he'd count. He liked to count, and I guess that's why he became a teacher. I don't know why really, but he would count and when he got to three, we could approach the bags in an orderly fashion and sort through the goodies.   Some things would sadly end up having to be trashed, and unfortunately it was usually the good stuff like the jelly donuts that lost some of their appeal when they found themselves at the bottom of the bag.   Despite this, however, we were able to salvage plenty of treasure.   Some would go to the big freezer on the porch, and others would be saved for tomorrow's 10 o'clock and 2 o'clock snacks.   We loved that job at the bakery, and it was such a treat for kids who were raised on pasta.

One day my dad came home with the devastating news that his company had changed their policy and that he could no longer bring home the trash.   It would have to go to the pig farm from now on.   We were devastated.   It just wasn't fair.   Why was it okay for the pigs and not for us?   Didn't they understand?   I wanted to write that store a letter and tell them how sad I was that they had taken away our bread and treats, but my dad advised against it.   It was what it was and there wasn't anything that could be done about it.   We'd just have to find another way.

A few years ago, I took a drive with my mom who is now in her late sixties.   She had come to take me out to lunch for my birthday, and over the course of the afternoon we reflected back on some great memories and some sad ones.   It was the first time that I can remember her ever talking about those days when she would go to the cabinet and all that was left was a bag of flour and a container of salt, and seven hungry sets of eyes staring up at her saying "Mom, I want a snack!"   She talked about how it hurt her to not be able to give us Easter baskets like other kids got or school pictures or some of the many things that we simply did without.   My mom told me that there were days when they didn't have any idea how they would come up with enough money for even a pasta dinner as the burden of raising seven kids weighed heavily upon both of their shoulders.

Hearing these confessions hurt my heart, and I suddenly wanted to go back and not be the ungrateful brat who demanded more.   I think of my mom's snack cabinet, the way she had to lock it up with a padlock to make the snacks last longer, and how my brothers one day thought it would be funny to unscrew the back off the cabinet and steal all the treats. I wonder now if Mom laughed or cried or both. What did my parents sacrifice in order to replenish those snacks? How many extra hours did my dad have to work to make up for a childhood prank that we still laugh about to this day?

I never worried about going hungry when I was a child, and hearing my mom's stories of those days made me marvel even more at how both my parents managed not only to survive but to keep the desperateness of the situation a secret from us all those years. They let us be kids and didn't trouble us with the fact that there was no money that week for groceries, or that the car going to the shop meant that we wouldn't see our father again for a while as he picked up extra night shifts. Though I didn't realize or appreciate it growing up, I had my very own Ma and Pa like Laura did and just never knew it. Instead of sugar cubes and potatoes with salt, I got slightly crushed, day old, yummy pastry from the bakery and a chocolate chip cookie on Easter Sunday. I was a lucky girl, and though my parents may have looked upon these things as a sign of their inadequacies, for me they were precious memories that I would have forever.

With the exception of the morning kiss goodbye, my parents were not overly affectionate people. We weren't huggers, seldom said things like "I love you," and didn't talk about emotional stuff. My dad could be a bit gruff and didn't say much, and I remember thinking sometimes that he was not a big fan of fatherhood. I knew he loved my mom, but there were times when I felt perhaps he could have done without the rest of us. As a kid, I didn't have any idea what it was like to work a sixteen hour day and then have to come home to seven kids running through the hallway and picking fights with each other. I didn't understand physical exhaustion or financial stress or how such things could fray the nerves and cause people to be edgy. I also never saw my parents as human beings. They were always just Mom and Dad, the people making the rules and telling me what I could and couldn't do. I didn't know what it was like to be in my twenties or my thirties and how unprepared I would have been at that age to be a parent or to suddenly have to give up on all my own dreams so that I could provide for my kids.

I remember comparing my mom to other moms who gave their kids excessive praise and showered them with affection, moms who made freshly baked cookies, and clothed their kids with the latest fashions. Though I didn't doubt her love, I didn't always recognize the way in which she chose to show it. I didn't understand back then how badly every parent wants their kids to be happy and to have the ability to give them the desires of their heart. I had no idea the amount of guilt and heartache one can feel as a grownup having to tell a five year old that you don't have enough money in your pocket for that ice cream that all the other kids are getting and to see sadness roll into your child's eyes. I can't imagine being a parent whose child equates not getting that ice cream with not being loved, and the added way in which that must sting a mother's heart.

As an adult, I am so grateful that I can see it now, the love that I didn't always understand or feel but that they both gave in their own ways. My parents weren't perfect, and there were times when they made parenting decisions that I imagine they may have come to regret. Given their deeply held religious convictions, they thought that it was wrong to offer praise to a child, because they believed it created a false sense of self. They didn't say things like, "I'm proud of you," because in their world, pride was a sin, and of course we all know that "pride cometh before the fall" as the Bible says. They were afraid that by saying "I'm proud of you for getting an A on that test," that perhaps it might cause us to develop an overly inflated ego which I guess they thought at the time may have caused us to turn to the dark side.

I imagine it was hard for them to balance being a parent and having their hearts telling them to do what parents do, while feeling their religion was commanding that they defy those natural parenting instincts out of obedience to a perceived mandate. I wonder sometimes if people with extreme ideologies that force them to choose between their children and their God face the same agony as described in the Bible when Abraham was told to offer up his son Isaac. I am not saying that my parents were extremists or claiming that my experience of not having my self-esteem stroked was anywhere close to the horror of placing a child on an altar with an intent to kill. What I am referring to is simply the way in which people of many religions can find themselves faced with that dilemma of having to choose between their belief systems and their children, and I can't imagine being in that position. Though I know my parents were often conflicted when it came to their religious convictions and their love for their children, and it was hard growing up knowing that if it ever came down to it, that they wouldn't choose you, I was still blessed to be given the parents that I have. When I hear of those who have disowned or abandoned their children, shutting them out of their lives forever whether due to religion, addiction, or just plain selfishness, I know that I am extremely fortunate. I was not an easy child to love at times, but they never gave up on me.

While I don't want to get too far off course by going down a theological rabbit hole, trying to find acceptance and approval was something I chased throughout my entire life which is why I broach this subject at all. My parents are good people who might actually take offense to my referring to them as "good," because they believe that none of us are "good" as we are all sinners. While I do not disagree with them that we are indeed all sinners as I haven't met a single individual who is perfect, I have also come to believe with all my heart that as a parent Himself who describes His children as "the apple of His eye" that God would not take offense to a parent whose love for their children boils over in such a way that they cannot contain the pride that they feel. I also believe that a child's view of God is often shaped by the way in which their parents see God. I wonder sometimes if they felt proud of us from time to time, and then felt like they had failed their God by having had such a thought or feeling. I also wonder if they ever felt like they were as much of a disappointment to their God as I sometimes felt I was both to Him and to them. Knowing what an awful way this is to live, it makes me sad to think they may have experienced it too.

Ami DeRienzo

CHAPTER 5

The conference call ended, and in the pit of my stomach I knew that life would never be quite the same. Though there was something within me that dared to hope, experience had taught me that things seldom work out to accommodate our hopes. I went down to the sales floor, determined to do what I had to do to get the job of the day done regardless of what may come.

As I walked across the checkout, a friendly face from the maintenance department greeted me and before we could talk about the reason for the service call, the conversation quickly shifted to the impending lay-offs. It was a brief conversation, interrupted suddenly when my eyes caught two figures walking toward us solemnly. In that moment, I knew who they were coming for and it was me. The same company that once told my father that he could no longer feed his children with the bakery trash, now several decades later was going to shake up my world once again and take away something that I loved.

After high school, I went to apply for a job at the grocery store where my dad worked all those nights in my childhood after he would get out of his "real job." I went there looking for something to help me get through college with no intention of ever staying, but here I was almost twenty years later, an assistant store manager who had made the painful climb up the ranks in what was an extremely competitive environment at the time.

Being one of the few females to achieve such a high ranking position in this male dominated industry, getting there had taken a great deal of sacrifice, late nights, and attempting to do everything with what felt like ten times the passion and effort than seemed to be required of my male counterparts. I worked an average of seventy hours a week, and when I wasn't working, I was at home in front of the computer making spreadsheets or trying to find a way to make my store a better place or to improve profitability for the company as a whole. While many of the guys I worked with were often out the door by 4:55 pm, most nights I was still there to greet the overnight crew and to make sure they had the tools and the help they needed to be successful. I loved every minute of it, finding that it gave me structure as well as a sense a purpose and belonging. While the job was never done, most of the time I could go home at night confident that I had done my best, and that there would always be tomorrow.

In fairness to my male counterparts, there were certainly those who believed in putting in late hours and going above and beyond as well. The difference, I guess, was the feeling that we were being judged by a different set of standards in order to get where we had gotten and to stay there. Perhaps it was all in my head, or maybe it had more to do with the fact that I was new to the position and they had been doing it for decades. Whatever the reason, I felt I was at a disadvantage due to my tendencies as a female not to raise my voice or bark commands. The company was moving in a direction in which management was expected to put company profits before people and squeeze every drop they could into the coffers. The managers who found acceptance and approval among the higher ups seemed to be the ones who had the ability to disconnect themselves from the needs of their associates, who knew how to play the game of sending blame downhill at the expense of their subordinates, and who had the ability to check out by 4:55 pm without ever looking back. Maybe I was a rebel or maybe it was that weakness in me that made me unable to step on ant houses as a child, but I struggled to comply with directives that I knew would ultimately be hurtful whether to my associates, my customers, or the company that I loved.

Now here they were. With only seventeen and a half years with the company, I was one of the least senior in my management role. The majority in my position were men with kids in college and families to support, while I was an unmarried female. I'm sure these things went into the decision making process when they chose which of us would be let go, or at least I hope it was something they considered. As brutal as it was for me, half of my torment was simply the knowledge that I wasn't the only one, that there were hundreds of others facing the same fate, maybe even some like my own father who had hungry children waiting at home depending on them.

About a week before this day, I had participated in a similar conference call in which we were told that there would be a manila envelope being delivered to the store and not to open it until we were given permission to do so. When the moment came, we were devastated to find the envelope contained a list of names of some of the best and most loyal associates we had, along with the instruction that we were to inform them that they were no longer employed. This list consisted of full-time individuals, many of whom had been with us for decades, and who were a part of our family. For the first time in my career, I hated the fact that I was a manager and would have to be a part of these individuals' memories of perhaps one of the worst days of their lives. This company directive would require us to call them into the office and tell them that the company deemed them disposable. Now this same company was coming for me, and I was being disposed of.

The human resources manager and district manager looked downward as they asked me if we could go up to the office. I led the way, knowing exactly what was coming. On the conference call moments earlier they had informed us that they would be visiting those today who were to be impacted by the management level lay-offs. Apparently, I must have been their first stop and I concluded that they had to have been participating in the call while sitting in their cars out in our parking lot as this is the only way they could have gotten there so quickly. Guess they were hoping that I might be the easiest, maybe because I was a girl who was unlikely to express anger or walk out in a rage.

I don't quite know how to describe that moment other than feeling like someone had kicked me in the stomach. It felt as if I might be sick, as if the world was suddenly spinning out of control, and that the demons from my past that I thought I had successfully buried could at any moment arise. The district manager read from the script that the company's lawyers had carefully crafted. It was a directive that had no doubt been given to them by their bosses and was likely the same directive I had been given the week before and ignored. My associates deserved more than a lawyer's script. They deserved someone who cared enough to at least be human and say this sucks, and I'm so sorry. Apparently this sentiment was not shared by the upper echelons or perhaps they were scared that they would be next. Their script was followed up by the human resources manager's "What questions do you have for us?"

While a part of me wanted to stand in defiance, to fight for my job and for the others so callously cast aside, instead I just wept, broken and resigning myself to defeat. I couldn't imagine life without my work family, without the job that motivated me to get out of bed every morning and that gave me purpose and direction in a life that had once seemed so pointless. It was all too familiar a scene of my life spinning out of control, of someone else calling the shots and making the decisions for me, of losing another family that I loved. There was nothing I could do but surrender.

In that moment, I thought of the woman on the checkout who applied for a job with us after being laid off from a company where she had worked for over thirty years. Suddenly I regretted my prior inability to empathize with the loss she was experiencing. While I had known many people who had mentioned to me in the past that they had been displaced, it was something that kind of passed through me, registering as a mere technicality and not a potentially life altering event that may have left them temporarily paralyzed or heartbroken. While I understood that sometimes a job was just a job, it suddenly became clear that losing a job can also feel a whole lot like you've lost your family and your reason for being. It made me sad that I never understood the grief that woman was going through when she would mention her old job. Perhaps I could have shown more compassion and respect for her loss, told her how sorry I was and simply been there for her. The weeks and months that followed took me back to another time when my life felt equally out of control.

Inescapable Madness - 1989

Barefoot, she danced endlessly to the sound of a cheap Walkman. Who knows if the music was ever on?

Marching up and down the hall, a young boy playing a harmonica in a long trench coat. The tunes went on late into the night...

A pre-adolescent, threatened with a tube, hours away from her home, fighting for control... Scared, alone, and self-starving...

A man who could only say, "I'm sorry! I'm sorry..." He broke down, and they formed a circle. Surrounded by strange voices and faces, he wasn't seen again for a very long time. Then, he was different...

A loud, annoying scream. A grown woman, refusing to get out of bed, refusing her lunch. When no one was looking, she left her wheelchair and stole some chocolate chip cookies. She wasn't supposed to be able to walk...

A mother of many kids, tough – a drill sergeant type. "I know my rights! Don't <u>you</u> tell me what to do!"

Thirteen, looking twenty... Ozzy stares down from the wall, photos of a child sacrifice to Satan. She is chasing a twenty-eight year old man...

An old man, quick as a whip, a humorous fellow, but only a thorn in his family's side... Medications made him seem funny, not humorous funny but sad. He couldn't remember where he was...

Her brother, killed in an auto accident. She came and went, no one seemed to know just where. When they could see her she was wonderful, but most of the time she simply fought just to stay...

A fifteen year old girl, uncertain of why, doesn't understand, misses her home and family, but knows she will never leave.

Who are you? Dancing in a trench coat, tied to a tube spitting apologies, stealing cookies while screaming independence, rebelling with a joke, losing your mind? Our pain, it's the same, and it's forever...

Ami DeRienzo

CHAPTER 6

The girl was dancing, literally dancing, up and down the hallway, as if she hadn't a care in the world. While this may not have seemed all that weird to me had I not been raised in a Baptist church where dancing was forbidden, the girl was wearing headphones that were obviously not plugged in as the cord dangled freely when she moved. She danced to music that apparently only she could hear. While I found her to be intriguing, I think she may have terrified my parents. As she danced away, she called out, "I'm fifteen too, you know!" It was the most bizarre thing, because there is no way she could have known my age. I concluded from this exchange that perhaps crazy folks saw each other in a way others couldn't and that our souls were somehow connected. She saw me, saw right through me, and that scared me far more than her rebellious dance routine.

The whole experience of getting there was a bit surreal, the phone call that was placed to my school, and the teacher who held me as I cried when she informed me that a bed had opened up at the psychiatric ward where I was to be admitted that afternoon. While we all knew that it was possible this day would come, there was something about the way the elevator doors shut behind us, the sign on the wall alerting us that this elevator would only stop on one floor, and the knowledge that this floor would be my new home for an indefinite period of time. We rang the buzzer, and were let in to the hospital ward by someone with a large set of keys, much like what I had seen in the movies being carried by prison guards.

The intake process had me rolling my eyes. As someone who had IQ tested at a college level when I was in the 7th grade, being asked if I knew who the President of the United States was made me laugh. For goodness sakes, I had worked as a volunteer on

President Reagan's campaign putting out yard signs around the neighborhood. Did I know who the President was? Ha! I remember thinking that I guess there must be different kinds of crazy... People like me and people who don't know who the President is...

It wasn't anything like what I had expected. In my mind, going to a hospital meant lying in bed where you had your very own TV. If you were particularly unlucky or poor like us, you would have to share your room with someone and be separated by a curtain. I had prayed that there would be an odd number of patients in the ward and that I would have my own room, but what I cared most about was being able to control the remote. I wasn't at all prepared for the fact that as a fifteen year old girl I would be sharing my room with three senior citizens, and there wasn't even a single television for us to fight over. As much as I came to love my new roommates and they were quick to adopt a grandmotherly role with me, the squeaking Depends was something that took getting used to. Having always had a particular sensitivity to noise, it was like scraping a chalkboard when one of them would make their way slowly across the room in the middle of the night. It just wasn't exactly the luxurious accommodations I was expecting, and it was readily apparent that there would definitely be no breakfast in bed at this place.

That first night was the hardest. As out of control as my life had felt up until that point in time, there had always been an escape route. If things got to be more than I could handle, there was that small comfort in knowing that I ultimately had control and could disappear one way or another. For the first time in my life, my emergency exits were all boarded up and my escape routes filled with patrol guards. I was stripped bare, left alone to experience every moment of my rawness without a means of release.

Unlike jail, which is fortunately an experience I've never had, they did not allow a phone call upon admittance. It was something I was told that I would have to earn. The same was true of visitation. Failure to comply with hospital rules and expectations would result in further isolation from the outside world. Unlike prison, there were no walks in the yard or group showers. They did have bars on the windows and a solitary confinement area, however, where some of my new friends would end up from time to time. The showers, although not group activities, might as well have been given the lack of privacy.

"Show us that body of yours!" **With this declaration, the camp counselor did the unforgivable and grabbed the towel that I had carefully wrapped around my wet and naked body, pulling it away and exposing me to all the girls in the room. While no one else seemed to share my issues of modesty and body shame, I was traumatized. I can't remember exactly what I said, but I'm guessing it was something like "I hate you, and hope you die!" Given the humiliation I felt and the rage inside me over this degrading experience, if I had a match, I probably could have burned her cabin to the ground for what she did and for what the other counselor failed to do by allowing it to happen. I did not want to spend another minute at this stupid camp. I was in the third grade.**

"Checks!" It was this that had brought me back to that day. As the nurse pulled the curtain back from the shower stall, all that shame and the feeling of being humiliated at camp returned. I hated that nasty woman who thought it was somehow okay to shame a little girl by exposing her publicly and the other adults who told me it was no big deal and to forget about it. Here we were, in another world created by grownups who thought it was okay to force a child to stand naked before them. In a place that was supposed to be safe, being spied on in the shower was not my idea of safety or a way to earn my trust.

As a newbie at the hospital, I spent my first week on fifteen minute checks which meant that every fifteen minutes a staff member would pop in and verify that I hadn't cut my wrists or hung myself yet. It didn't matter if I was in the shower or sitting on the toilet, if it was time then it was time. Having come from a family of seven kids, I wasn't used to a great deal of privacy, but I could never get used to the invasiveness of checks. In this regard, the hospital felt like another perpetrator, another person or place that lured me into a false sense of safety only to confirm to me that there was no place I could go to be free of the monsters.

I didn't like being surprised, and to this day, I like what I like, and it is hard for me to deviate from my comfort zones. There are about ten meals that I like, and that is what I will eat. There are a handful of restaurants that I am comfortable going to, and that is where I go. There are certain people and social situations that I feel safe in, and going outside that circle often causes severe anxiety that is hard to explain to people who don't understand. The hospital was new and unfamiliar territory surrounded by strangers, and I was stripped of any decision making capabilities. I couldn't choose my meals or decide when to go to bed. Although the accommodations were nicer than prison being that I wasn't afraid of being knifed by the eighty-five year old sleeping next to me, there were still a lot of similarities, right down to the regimented routines and barred windows.

One saving grace in the hospital for me was that I was still able to smoke and to do so indoors. This was of course back in the 80s when it was still acceptable to smoke in hospitals and even grocery stores. It's hard to imagine such a thing in today's world, but that was the way things were. Despite their strip search and high tech security, I also took great pride in knowing that I had smuggled in a straight edge razor blade and a joint without their knowledge, just in case things got to be too much.   It took me a couple weeks, but I eventually felt safe enough that I turned this contraband over to my therapist as a trust offering.

My therapist was Dr. White, a child psychiatrist that I began seeing twice a week while in my early teens after I had already made thirteen suicide attempts and had been cutting daily for years. My relationship with Dr. White spanned over the course of approximately ten years off and on, and during that time she kept me alive. On more than one occasion, she was woken in the middle of the night and came running to my rescue. As one of her first patients when she started her practice, we had a special relationship that meant the world to me, and I am convinced that I would not have made it without her. She became my reason to live, my motivation to hang on when there was nothing else I could hang on to. I kept a countdown clock, and could tell you at any moment how many days, minutes, and seconds until my next appointment. It was Dr. White who first encouraged me to write about my feelings in a journal when I could not find the words to express myself verbally. Over the many years of therapy, I kept journals for her that she would read during our sessions, journals that still sit in a box in my attic as evidence of a life that sometimes feels as if it was lived by someone else.

Journal Entry – 3/23/1989

There is so much I don't understand, so many questions, so many fears. I fear death and yet I fear life even more. I fear people, to trust and to give them love. I'm beginning to feel things, loneliness, pain, fear... It's so scary. I wish I could keep up a wall around my heart at all times, not letting anyone in and not letting anything out. There used to be a wall, but it's beginning to fall piece by piece. I feel so naked and vulnerable.

There are so many thoughts and feelings, so much anger and love, everything begins to blur into one. Sometimes I know my thoughts. I understand them. Other times I catch a glimpse of them as though they were portrayed on a flashing screen. I can't keep up and I don't know what they mean.

I'm so scared I'll lose my mind, my control, my security. There is so much crazy stuff going on in my head. I don't want anyone to see when it all comes out. The reality still hasn't set in that I am actually here. It all feels like a dream. I can't believe all the bad things that I've done. It makes me sick just to think of it all. I don't think it was me. It couldn't have been...

CHAPTER 7

I didn't mean to do it. Can't remember exactly how old I was, but I couldn't have been more than eight or nine. I was the type of kid who spent hours trying to help the ants build their homes and would relocate bugs from indoors to outdoors, hoping to protect them from humans who may wish to do them harm. When I saw the baby bird, all I could think was that it needed me. It was all alone, no mommy or daddy in sight, letting out a mournful cry or so the bleating sounded to me. It needed food, water, someone who would take care of it and love it in a way I knew I could. I had no idea that what I was about to do was wrong. I never meant to cause it any harm.

When I woke that morning and took off for another adventure on my bike around the neighborhood in Gorham, I had no way of knowing that I was about to make a forever memory. I didn't know that my actions that day would come to haunt me into my adult years. But here I sit, thirty-five years later, sharing the story of a baby bird that I killed and whose memory has become a part of me.

In many ways, this bird's story was my own story, perhaps not in reality, but it was how I felt back then and the creature with whom I most identified. Perhaps I was an overly dramatic kid, maybe it was just the way I was wired, but when I saw that baby bird, there was an instant feeling of connection. I felt its sadness and the feeling of abandonment that I assumed it must be experiencing having been left all alone in that nest. Just as I was searching for a savior to rescue me from the creeping feeling of my own darkness, this little creature was searching for someone too. We were meant to find each other. I would be to that bird what I so wanted someone to be for me.

As I picked it up and cupped it into my little girl hands, I remember a feeling of joy and love come upon me. I was excited to step into our driveway, eager to show off my new friend to my mom and siblings. Before I had reached the door, however, my grand delusions of self-worth were shattered when my older sister saw me coming and confronted me in anger with a look of disgust.

"What have you done?!? You know you might as well have killed that bird because its mom is never coming back now cause of you! You're so stupid!"

After all these years, I'm not sure if those really were her words or if that is simply what I heard in my head. She went on to explain to my traumatized brain that the mama bird would smell my ugly human stink and would never come back now for her baby, that the bird's mom probably had just run out to get some food, but now would never come back. For the child who could not bear the guilt of damaging an ant house, this was just too much. Devastated, I remember crying my eyes out, begging God not to ruin this little creature's life because of me. I brought it back to its nest and prayed with everything I had that the mama would come back. She never did, and despite my best efforts, the baby bird died the next day. And so there I was, a murderer before the age of ten, living with that guilt but also knowing that I caused that poor little bird to become a victim of the ultimate betrayal, being abandoned by its mom. I could not imagine a greater crime, going from savior to monster, protector to perpetrator. This experience would haunt me and became the subject of projection for many years in psychotherapy.

"Ami, what are feeling right now? What's going on?"

"Thinking about the bird..."

"Do you think it's almost ready to fly?"

"No... I think I need to kill it... The bird needs to die..."

Journal Entry – 3/24/1989

All that's left is emptiness. Why am I here? I feel so cold, inside and out. Everything I had has been taken away, and now I have nothing. I don't understand why so many people have been sending cards and bright thoughts. They are the same ones who used to fear me. They all have their own walls and feel safe now that I am behind mine. This hospital has big, thick walls. I suppose they are here for security, protection. I feel as though I were hiding behind these walls.

I've tried so hard to tell them that the cutting thing is no big deal, but they just won't believe me. I don't understand why they didn't help me back a few years ago when I needed it, back when I was younger and innocent. I've hardened to so much now. I don't want to be hard, especially callous to others needs, but it just seems to be happening and there's nothing I can do to stop it. I've lost control over everything now. There's just no way that they will ever let me live a life of my own. Let someone else make the decisions so you don't screw everything up. I'm so scared of screwing everything up. I don't want people to hate me for my evil thoughts and feelings. I'm so scared they'll all leave me when they see through my disguises. I don't want anyone getting into my mind. God, what will they find?

Journal Entry – 11/16/1992

i don't know why
the sight of blood
offers such satisfaction
or the blistering
of burnt flesh
turns me on

i know
they don't understand
and i don't know
how to tell them
it's nothing serious

it is all just a way
to entertain myself
and conserve resources
more valuable
than i

CHAPTER 8

It was one of my favorite places. I went there often to be alone and to write in my journal. It was about a half a mile from our home in Gorham, a trail that ran off the end of a dirt road and then went on for miles through a wooded area. It was a peaceful place. One time, as I sat writing while sitting on a fallen log, a moose came right up to where I was. We stared into each other's eyes, as if we could see our respective souls. This time, however, I wasn't going there to commune with nature or to write. I went there because I thought it would be a good place to die.

My actions were robotic. It felt as if I was no longer in my body and something else much more sinister had taken over. This wasn't the first time I had attempted to end my life, but it was certainly the most dramatic method I had chosen. In the past I had always opted for pills. The first time we had been on a family vacation up in Rumney, New Hampshire staying in a cabin at a Bible retreat. I had gone off on my own and gotten lost in the mountains for close to eight hours, not knowing if and how I would ever find my way back, and it was a terrifying experience. When I did return, I discovered that no one was there and that they'd all left for church without me. I wondered if they had even noticed that I was gone. I went into a small room in the cabin, locked the door behind me, and proceeded to down an entire bottle of aspirin with a six pack of a special soda they no longer make that had twice the sugar and caffeine. I wrote a short suicide note addressed to someone who I admired and who was kind to me at our church named Mara and went to sleep. My parents had to kick in the door to the room when they got home, and I was out for a couple days recovering from that first stint. I was eleven.

Throughout junior high school, I made numerous feeble attempts to end my life, once landing in the emergency room to have my stomach pumped. This day in the woods, though, was different. This was my first truly bold attempt that involved a complete disconnect from my body. I found the right spot which was an area off the trail that I thought would be a good place to die. I began to collect large rocks and placed them in a body sized circle, then filled the circle with leaves and brush. When I finished preparing my altar, I sat down in the middle of it. Using my cigarette lighter, I set fire to the brush and watched as the flames began to engulf me. My jeans caught fire, and I could smell the flesh on the back of my legs burning. Though I was capable of smell, I could not feel. I was numb, both mentally and physically.

My jeans were almost completely gone before I suddenly woke from my haze. The fire was starting to spread beyond the circle, threatening to consume the beautiful woods that had provided me such comfort. Though I cared little for my own survival, I did not want to be responsible for destroying another thing that I loved. My grandfather... The baby bird... They were enough. I couldn't kill this beautiful sanctuary too. I jumped up with only minutes to spare before the situation would have been completely out of hand. After extinguishing what remained of my jeans so as not to spread the flames further, I chased after the fire that was quickly spreading throughout the surrounding dry brush. I suppose I could have stuck around after saving the forest and found a way to build a proper fire pit and done it right. Not sure exactly why I didn't, other than the fact that once the adrenaline wore off the burnt flesh on the back of my legs was starting to hurt.

It was slow going getting back to the house where I made up an absurd story to explain why I had no pants from the thighs on down and why there was melted jean material sunken into my flesh. There is nothing quite like the pain of when your skin is gone and your insides are exposed, or having to use a tweezer to try to fish out errant pieces of cloth that think they are now a part of you. I guess perhaps it is like that pain you feel when you have a horrible toothache due to an exposed nerve and every time something hot, cold, or otherwise touches it, you feel it throughout your entire body. The lower half of my right leg became one giant toothache for several weeks as I hobbled along on crutches. I think

I told them I fell asleep smoking a cigarette and caught the grass on fire. Getting in trouble for smoking was a much better alternative than getting locked up for being crazy. Pretty sure my therapist didn't buy it, but we went on for a few more weeks just the same.

Perhaps the fire was when she put my name on the hospital waiting list. She had warned me several times before that it could happen. Since the sixth grade, I had been an avid cutter. Back in those days it was virtually unheard of, but I guess now it has become quite common. What I would do is take a straight edge razor blade, the type people in retail use in case cutters for opening boxes, and would use it to cut my arms, my legs, my chest, wherever there was still room and where it could easily be hidden by clothing. It became one of my first addictions, second only to smoking which I also started in the sixth grade.

Cutting is one of those things people do that I think sometimes may be misunderstood, and I guess the same can be said for just about any addiction or self-destructive behavior. Of course I can only share my experiences and what it was for me which could be entirely different than what it may be for someone else. For me, cutting was a coping mechanism, much like biting my nails, smoking, or chewing gum. It was a means of self-soothing, a release, like that glass of wine that someone may have after a long day at work. At the same time, it was a means of survival. It was the O'Doul's that is consumed by the alcoholic trying to get sober or the tread mill in the winter for the obsessive runner unfortunate enough to live in a climate like Maine's.

The first time I picked up a knife and cut my wrists, I was doing what many young kids do which was a feeble attempt to kill myself. Without the existence and aid of Google, I had no way of knowing the correct way to commit suicide and did it all wrong. What that moment did for me, however, was expose me to the incredible rush that came with watching myself bleed. What I also experienced in that moment was an ability to feel something other than the feeling of emptiness that seemed to be taking over. It felt good to feel something tangible, something real, and something that didn't hurt anywhere near as much as the sadness in my head.

After that first attempt, the day when I crossed that line and took the action to scar my body, from there on out it was easy. When I needed to feel something, I would cut. When I was feeling anxious or sad or disappointed or alone, I would cut. It didn't take long to discover that razor blades were far easier to manage than a kitchen knife. You could take them anywhere, and they were easy to hide. I found that razor blades also made cutting far more efficient and effortless. Once I realized that it would be highly unlikely that cutting would result in death, it became my pacifier, my way to avoid suicide by having an alternate release.

I was a private cutter, one who hid their scars and did not want others to know what was happening. Although many dismiss suicide attempts and other self-destructive acts as a means of seeking attention or manipulation, this was never a conscience intention on my part, and I can't imagine any kid picking up a razor blade and thinking to themselves, "Man, this looks like a great way to get noticed!" As bizarre as it may seem to those who haven't been there, I actually thought of cutting as a loving act. Despite my feeling of disconnection to the people and the world around me, I did love my family and others in my life. In my heart I knew that to commit suicide would be selfish and hurtful. People had been telling me that for years and the thought of hurting someone I loved came with a tremendous amount of guilt. I wanted to die, but I didn't want anyone else to suffer. I just wanted to put an end to my own suffering. For me, cutting was a way to protect those I cared about from having to bury me or from having to spend their lives wondering if it was their fault or if there was something they could have done. I was cutting so I wouldn't have to die. I realize that may not make sense to anyone but me, but it was how I felt. For me, cutting was my way of expressing love for the people in my life, accepting an alternative that I thought would be less painful for them than what I really wanted to do.

Despite my good intentions, when the numerous scars on my body were discovered, the rest of the world didn't see my coping mechanism in quite the same way as I did. There were interventions from friends and teachers from my school, as well as threats of institutionalization from mental health professionals and DHS. It was clear to me that if I were to survive I would need to come up with a better way to not kill myself.

CHAPTER 9

It was a hot summer day and my parents loaded us into the car to make the two hour journey to my grandparents' house in Massachusetts. While we didn't make the trip often, it was Father's Day weekend in 1983, a month before my tenth birthday. We were going to spend the day with my father's family, and in case my last name doesn't give it away, this was the Italian side of my heritage. This get together was like many others before it, done in true Italian fashion. While the Irish have their whiskey and pints, we Italians have our wine and good food. While neither of my parents ever drank, the most popular game at Grandma's house was searching for Grandma's wine. It seemed that at least once every fifteen minutes or so, everything would stop and Grandma would call out, "Where's my wine???" and all us kids would scramble and begin the search. I quickly learned that the best place to look was in her hand. I used to think it was the drink, but as I've begun to age and am constantly looking for the glasses that are on my face, I've come to think that perhaps it is in our genetic makeup.

Going to Grandma's was such fun growing up. She made us each feel as if we were the most important person on the planet, though at times I think she was a little partial to the boys. From the moment we walked in the door, she would fill our bellies with every imaginable treat from homemade Italian cookies to platefuls of manicottis, meatballs, and sausage. Every meal came with about fourteen courses and each one was just as good as the one before it. She would even pack us up leftovers to make sure we didn't starve on the way home. If I had a wish for children everywhere, it would be that they could know and experience the love of an Italian grandmother like the one I had. She was something else.

Besides all the wonderful food, the smothering of hugs and kisses, and the entertainment provided by a multitude of great aunts who drank too much wine, there were also uncles that added to the life of the party. Though the *Sopranos* didn't exist back then, my great uncles could have easily been cast for a role in the show. One of my favorite memories is of the money rolls that they would take out of their pockets and use to impress our young minds. Following their inspiration, I remember collecting dollar bills until I had enough to make a roll of my own and would carry it around, pretending to be a gangster.

Until I was nine and almost ten, going to Grandma's was one of my favorite adventures. They had an in-ground pool where we learned to swim and that provided hours of entertainment every summer. My grandma would worry like only an Italian grandmother could about that pool and was obsessed with making sure the kids were never out there alone. Years earlier, when I was about six, we were not alone. On that day, my grandma was inside the house taking care of guests, and likely searching for her wine. My grandfather sat in the lawn chair beside the pool, chatting with other relatives and watching us swim. Unlike my grandma who coddled and babied us in a way that we all enjoyed, Grandpa had a different way of showing affection and seemed to take great pleasure in teasing us. For whatever reason, he used to call my little sister Mikey in an effort to get her going, perhaps because she was the most feminine one of the bunch, and he enjoyed watching her protest, insisting that she was girl and not a boy. It was obvious that he loved his grandkids, but his ways of showing it were different from Grandma's. He could be a little gruff with the grownups, but almost never showed this side to us kids.

I was out in the pool that day when I was nine and almost ten with several of my siblings As we played, Beth and Matt decided to experiment using the diving board, and before long they were jumping like champs into the water while I continued to cling to the side of the pool, holding on to the cement edges for dear life. As they swam back and forth in the deep end, I remained cautious. I had almost drowned in this pool many years earlier and had been unable to get over my phobia or attempt swimming since.

From the sidelines, my grandfather was calling out to me, teasing me for being a chicken and not being as good as my brother and sister were. My grandfather had been there four years earlier, had seen that I almost drown and had to be rescued by a fully clothed stranger. How could he be so cruel? How could he not understand why I was afraid? He was laughing at my fear, and I remember getting so angry that I literally thought the words "drop dead." As horrible as that sounds, for whatever reason the phrase seemed to be a fad in the eighties. Doesn't make it any better, but it was not so much that I was a little psychopath wishing to murder my grandfather. It was really just an inappropriate expression of anger at a moment when my feelings were hurt.

As he was teasing me, all I could think of was the day that I almost drown and how I had seen his face laughing as I gasped for air. Was he sitting in that same exact chair now where he watched me go under and is he laughing at me again? Of course in my head I knew that my grandpa would not intentionally let me drown, but he was there. He knew what happened to me and why I was afraid to swim. While I know he meant no harm with his teasing and that he loved his grandkids immensely, as a little girl I did not understand. I thought he was being cruel, and in that moment, I wished him dead.

Two days after my unbridled anger, the phone rang and I could tell there was something wrong. My mom took my dad out on the porch and told us to stay inside. I watched through the door window, eager to know what was going on. I remember the way my father's head slumped down, how my mom wrapped her arms around him. I remember the tears that ran down his face, tears I had never witnessed in my near ten years of life with the exception of an occasional *Little House on the Prairie* episode. My dad, the man of few words and little emotion, was broken. I was terrified.

He eventually left the porch and took a walk around the yard while my Mom came back in and told me what was going on. My grandfather had dropped dead of a heart attack. He was gone. Grandpa was gone and Daddy was crying. My poor Grandma... I immediately thought of her and how sad she must be, and that it was my fault. I killed Grandpa. I ran off up to my room to be alone as I had some business to take care of with God.

In the next hour, I prayed like I had been taught, confessing my sin of having had evil thoughts. I knew the story of Jesus's friend Lazarus who died and then came back to life, and I believed with all my heart that once I apologized to God for my wickedness that Grandpa would be alright. After my prayer session, I was so confident that God would fix things that I put a smile on my face and went downstairs to inform my parents that I had taken care of it and that God promised me that Grandpa would come back in three days. When we made the solemn journey down to Massachusetts and arrived at Grandma's, I told her the same thing. Grandpa wasn't really dead. God just had to punish me for my bad thoughts, but he'd be coming back soon. I was so convinced having faith only a child can have. This was my first experience with human death, and all I knew were the Bible stories. It worked for Lazarus and for Jesus. Of course it would work for Grandpa!

As the days and weeks went by, not only did I lose my faith, but I also became convinced that I was the wickedest child to have ever existed. Who kills their own grandpa?!? If a God who loves and forgives everyone couldn't forgive me, then I had to rank right up there with Satan himself. I was a murderer. I was evil, and I deserved to die. God made it clear to me that I was not worthy of forgiveness. It also became clear to me that I had the power to kill with my thoughts. From here on out, I could not think bad things or there would be devastating consequences. I could not command anyone to drop dead ever again unless I really meant it. I became terrified of my own power, my own mind, and the entity that was once my own God. This hadn't been the first time I had killed, but I prayed it would be the last. I now had the blood of both my grandpa and that baby bird on my hands. This all took place shortly before I was about to transition to a new school, leaving behind a childhood of familiarity and safe places and exchanging them for a frightening journey into the unknown. The kid who used to like bananas and building forts was replaced with an angry and withdrawn preadolescent.

The Italian Grandparents (Center), Back: Beth, Dad, David & Mom, Front: Ami (9), John, Sandy & Matt

Though you can't see him, baby brother Joey is in Mom's tummy...

CHAPTER 10

Middle school and junior high can be the most miserable, wretched times, or at least that was my experience. In my grammar school days, things had been simple. Though there were occasions when I got sent to the principal's office for silly things like giving that kid a black eye, or times when I may have felt rejected by my peers, I had still been in a small private school where you couldn't get lost, literally or figuratively. When I was about to start fifth grade, my mom decided she was going to home school all seven of us due to the high cost of private school. This was a year of transition for me as I was leaving behind the friends and familiarity of the only school I'd known, while at the same time beginning to experience the challenges of preadolescence. Fifth grade was the year when I started to rage, and sixth grade was when I began to despair.

I had no idea where the anger was coming from, but it seemed to take over my body in the same uncontrollable manner as did the physical changes brought on by puberty. I remember waking up and feeling like I was going to explode for no reason at all. There was a rage inside me with absolutely nowhere to go. I couldn't explain or make sense of it. It wasn't logical or rational. It just was. I remember one day taking a baseball bat and swinging it for about five minutes straight, bashing it against the side of a tree. As my mom watched out the window, she later confessed that she was afraid of my anger and the vengeance with which I swung that bat. As a girl, it was not okay to yell or get in fist fights or express anger the way my brothers did. Despite the occasional instances in which the rage boiled over and I couldn't help myself, most of my anger was internalized. Instead of reaching out and punching someone in the face, those violent impulses that I seemed unable to control came out in other ways. I had no desire to hurt anyone, and there was a part of me that knew the feelings were irrational and unjustified. Regardless, there was no way to combat emotion with logic at this time in my life. The feelings were too intense and powerful as the hormones raged. When a baseball bat wouldn't do, I found some relief pounding my fists into a hard surface, causing my knuckles to swell and sometimes bleed. As someone who is now in my forties with arthritic joints, I can tell you that this is not something I would recommend as you may need those knuckles someday.

By the time fifth grade came to an end, my parents concluded that perhaps homeschooling wasn't quite as ideal a solution as it had originally sounded. They decided to send us to the public school in Gorham, a place where my awkwardness seemed to fully blossom. Unlike my prior school where the kids were more like siblings than classmates, this place was an entirely different environment. I didn't know anyone, and unfortunately lacked the social skills to make friends easily. I don't know what labels kids use today, but back then the schools were all divided into several factions that we called clicks. There were geeks, burnouts, jocks, brains, and preps. When I first arrived, there was no doubt in my mind that the only place I was going to stand a chance of acceptance would be with the geeks. I was a gawky kid, dressed in second-hand clothes that hadn't been cool for at least a decade, and I was cursed with early development causing me to stand out even more from my peers. People weren't exactly beating down my door to get to know the new kid, but those who did extend an olive branch or spoke to me kindly meant the world to me, even if it was only half a smile or not picking me last in gym class.

Though it took a while, eventually I was invited to hang out with two girls that had been friends with each other since childhood. Labeling them now feels so mean, but if they were to be described based on their standing in the school, they would have fallen into the "geek" category simply because they existed as outsiders, rejected by the cool kids. They let me be their friend for a couple months until one day at recess, they turned on me and said that they'd been talking and decided they liked it better when there was only two of them instead of three. I was devastated... Though I didn't feel terribly close to either of them, it was still a bit of a blow to be rejected by the people that other people reject. It made me question what that said about where I stood in the pecking order of popularity. I didn't realize there was a level below geek, but there obviously was, and I was it. I was on my own.

Fortunately for me, they were not the only two girls in the school willing to take a chance on a newbie. Before long, I met two wonderful girls who for the remainder of sixth grade became my BFFs. They were from the prep crowd, but there was something different about them. They were kind and compassionate with no sign of snobbery or entitlement, just two good people who weren't threatened by taking me in as a third wheel. My friend Cheryl and her redheaded sidekick Janice saved me in sixth grade from completely giving up. While I never felt as if I fit in with the rest of their crowd, when I was with the two of them, I felt as if maybe things could be okay after all. Without internet or cell phones back in those days, one of the most popular means of communication was through the passing of notes. To this day, somewhere in a box in either my basement or attic is a stash of handwritten notes from over thirty years ago all signed "Love Ya! DNQ!" For those not familiar with the acronym because you are obviously not in your forties, it stood for "Dearly Not Queerly" which was important for us to assert back in those days lest anyone get the wrong idea. These little notes I received from my new BFFs meant the world to me, so much so that I have held on to them all these years...

In recent days, my life partner and I have been watching a series on Netflix entitled *Thirteen Reasons Why*. The show is about a young girl who commits suicide and leaves behind a recording that identifies thirteen individuals whose actions contributed to her ultimate decision to end her life. As I've watched, I can't help but think how much I would love to write a similar story entitled *Thirteen Reasons Why Not*. If I were to do so, Janice and Cheryl would have made the cut as being individuals whose small acts of kindness unbeknownst to them ultimately played a role in saving my life. I think back as to how things could have been different had they not accepted me or if they had chosen to be cruel. They were critical to my survival in those days, and I could not imagine having gotten through middle school without them.

Though we eventually grew apart when we moved on to junior high and high school, we had some fun times together in sixth grade. One of my favorite memories is of the talent show that I was too chicken and lacking talent to participate in, but I remember beaming with pride as I watched my new friends do their dance routines to Prince and Cyndi Lauper. Being accepted by Cheryl and Janice opened up another world for me as it seemed to give others permission to look upon me as perhaps worthy of friendship. As I got to know other kids, I dreamed of a day when we would no longer have to be segregated by labels and could see that we weren't any different from each other. I became friends with individuals from different clicks and couldn't imagine ever having to choose one group over another. The very idea of it caused me great stress and anxiety. I went from being a kid with no friends at all to worrying about what I would do if I suddenly had too many friends from different groups and was somehow forced to choose.

By the time I hit junior high, I had begun withdrawing further into myself, overwhelmed by the idea of trying to make it all fit when I simply didn't fit. As a smoker, I started hanging out more with the friends they labeled burnouts, which is how I really got to know my new friend Theresa. We also shared biology class together where as my partner she saved me from ever having to do the dirty work, things that made my stomach churn even to watch like mutilating those poor frogs. Theresa was someone who also would have landed in an episode of my *Thirteen Reasons Why Not* series. She became my best friend in junior high and high school, helping me through many difficult times. Theresa was the girl who always had my back.

trying too hard

maybe that's it

i'm trying too hard

that's why no one wants me

that's why they are laughing

trying too hard

that's it

chill out

take a sedative

then maybe

someone will want me

maybe someday

when i quit trying

in a coma

then

they'll want me

dead.

Ami DeRienzo

CHAPTER 11

"Class, your attention please, or I will break your knees!"

She must have been about four and a half feet tall, but if you knew her, she was one of those people who came across as a giant. Her small frame, short hair style, and Canadian accent made her stand out from the other teachers at Shaw Junior High School as well as her larger than life personality. We didn't know quite what to make of her when the school year began. There were a lot of terrified faces that first week of seventh grade as she made clear that her expectations were unlike anything we had been exposed to in middle school. This lady was going to be tough, and she didn't miss a beat. You would not want to be the kid that fell asleep in this class, not that you ever could. She had a way of making everything interesting.

Muttering under one's breath or groaning about anything was not tolerated. She expected us to work hard and to be successful. It didn't matter to her if we were one of the privileged or the kid getting free lunch, we were all the same, all capable of greatness and of achieving our dreams. To hear someone say they believed in me and to actually be convinced that they meant it, well that was what made her different. There was no doubt that she was tough, perhaps the toughest teacher I ever encountered, but it was because she wanted to squeeze the very best out of us and show us what we could do.

We had just finished up our unit on *The Diary of Anne Frank* and were given a major assignment which involved writing a lengthy essay processing what we had just read. The essay I had turned in was about twenty pages long, but then again those were the days when REALLY BIG handwriting was in style. Not only did we use wide-ruled, lined paper, but our letters seldom stayed between the lines, and it was not uncommon to find you could only fit about eight words to a line. I remember spending countless hours trying to mimic my friends' handwriting that I thought was so beautiful. Despite my best efforts, I hated my writing and like everything else in my world, I felt I couldn't do anything as well as everyone around me did. Regardless, the twenty page paper was something that I worked hard on for her, wanting to please her in a way that I had never been motivated by any teacher before or since. After her daily threat of breaking our knees, Ms. Fleming informed us that she had graded our papers, and it was as if all the air was sucked out of the room as we awaited her judgment.

Writing about Anne Frank had come easy as the book touched my heart. Like Laura Ingalls, Anne was an inspiration that made me want to experience life in a way I hadn't, to break out of the prison that was my own body, and to connect like others around me seemed capable of doing. As Anne wrote about her desire to learn to dance and to unleash the free spirit that existed within her, I too longed for that freedom to let loose and become someone I had never been allowed to be. This is what my essay was about, wanting to learn how to embrace life with the passion of Anne Frank regardless of circumstance, fears, and personal limitations.

"One of you went above and beyond on this assignment. In fact, it was one of the best papers I have ever read, something I would expect from a college student. With Ami's permission, I'm going to read it to you now..."

I couldn't breathe. She was pleased with me. I had done well, and she was proud. It was as if in that moment every bit of sadness was momentarily suspended, and I was living someone else's life. I don't remember her reading the essay or what happened during the remainder of the class. I do remember, however, that great big A+++++ that she had written across the top of the page with a smiley face. It was one of the happiest moments in my life. It didn't matter to me what the other kids thought or if they would laugh at me behind my back. All I needed was her approval, and she had given it.

Throughout the remainder of seventh grade, Ms. Fleming became a special friend and mentor. She often gave up her free period to sit with me, helping to make school a safe place. I let her into my world through my writing, and she in turn took me under her wing and helped me to survive through one of my most difficult years. She offered me a glimmer of light at the end of the darkness. Even after the school year ended, she was there for me, and I will always be grateful for the way in which she helped to shape my dreams during that time of vulnerability.

Though Ms. Fleming was still in the building when I moved on to eighth grade, it wasn't the same not seeing her on a daily basis. I couldn't find that special connection we had shared with my new teachers, and again felt terribly alone. Due to my disdain for verb conjugation, I spent a good portion of eighth grade in detention. Although I had no problem composing an actual sentence using correct verb tenses, I found the idea of memorizing endless verbs and creating lists and diagrams to be ridiculous. I didn't understand why my English teacher of all people didn't understand that words were meant to exist in a sentence and not a diagram. In my efforts of protest and desire to take a stand against the lunacy, I found myself in an adversarial relationship with an instructor who held the power of detention, and that is how I spent a good part of the year as a radical protester of verbs. Maybe one of those hours spent with her after school actually saved me from some unknown tragedy that was waiting for me outside the door. Regardless, I still stand by my convictions with regard to verb conjugation.

Though I had some great friends who I hung out with, I found it difficult to relate to my peers in junior high. The cutting continued and when it wasn't enough, I would burn myself with cigarettes, leaving permanent scars on my body. I would literally take an entire cigarette and watch it burn its full length down into my skin so I could feel something. I became obsessed with Pink Floyd, relating all too much to the lyrics of songs like "Comfortably Numb" and "The Trial." It took me until my sophomore year when I met Miss A to find a teacher surrogate to fill the void left by Ms. Fleming. While there were many teachers who cared and touched my life in different ways, these two went far above the call of duty in terms of the love and support they gave over the years for which I will be forever grateful. We had special relationships that were sometimes confused by what I came to learn was a mental health defect in my brain, causing me to have more demanding and intense relationships than the average person. Despite this, they dealt with my idiosyncrasies and were there supporting me through some incredibly rough years.

for 25 years this sadness has been mine
i cannot remember the other five years
even the happiest of times shrouded
a bubble waiting to burst
therapy, introspection, religion
and still i am here
feeling as if i were dropped on the wrong planet
a stranger in the most unfamiliar of places
is it me, or is it something bigger
have i sabotaged myself so many times
that i no longer recognize the signs
or am i powerless
the victim of something greater than myself
why do i want to cry…

CHAPTER 12

"Ami, your tutor is here to see you..."

With this announcement, the nurse stepped aside, and there in the door frame stood my English teacher Miss A. My face lit up, as she in turn grinned back at me. The nurse eyed us both with suspicion, likely questioning whether she had missed something that perhaps should have been obvious. As someone who was only in her twenties at the time, Miss A could easily be mistaken for a teenager herself and didn't project the image of a typical high school teacher. After looking her up and down, the nurse obviously felt the need to prove she had done her due diligence from a security perspective, as she proceeded to question her.

"You really are her tutor, correct?"

I'm guessing teenagers weren't usually grinning from ear to ear when they were told it was time to do their studies, which must have been what raised the nurse's spidey-senses. I was not allowed visitors, so had Miss A not identified herself as my tutor, there is no way she would have gotten through the door. After the nurse finally left us alone, my dear friend and mentor confessed that she had wanted to visit and that she had volunteered to be my tutor as it was her only way in. We sat together on my bed like a couple of old friends who hadn't seen each other in ages. When the nurse came back later doing checks and saw that we did not appear to be engaged in anything academic, her suspicion increased, but she let it go. For that hour, Miss A made me the happiest girl on the ward, making me laugh and remembering all the reasons why I loved her.

I imagine most people can look back and reflect on those in their lives who had an impact, people who inspired them or served as a mentor along the way. My guess is that these kind of relationships can be strong and significant for everyone. I make assumptions about what it is like for the average person, but because my brain is wired a little differently, I don't really know. For me, the influential people in my life were more than just mentors or adults that I looked up to. They were my heroes. They were people who could do no wrong and who I looked up to with complete love and adoration. Miss A was one of three heroes who kept me alive throughout my adolescent years and the importance of her role in my life during this time was second only to my therapist Dr. White. These individuals chose to give of themselves far above and beyond what any teacher or therapist is expected to give, and in doing so, I have no doubt that they saved me. Of course there were many more than three people who played a significant role in keeping me safe over the years and who helped get me through the darkest times in my life (far too many to ever start naming), but without the love of my therapist, my seventh grade literature teacher, and Miss A, I am quite certain I would not be here today.

My attachment and dependence upon them was not "normal" in the sense that most people have relationships. In my mind, they walked on water and were goddesses who could do no wrong. They were smart and funny and beautiful and kind, and I became obsessed in what I now can see was an unhealthy manner as I've come to understand my own mental illness. It was that feeling you get when you are in love and can't stop the smile from coming across your face every time you see or even think about someone. It was complete and utter adoration. While I didn't attach anything romantic or sexual in meaning to my infatuation at the time, my feelings could quite easily be described as being similar to a monstrous, obsessive crush. It was the same love I had for my best friend in childhood. Being around them made me feel safe and joyful, free to be who I was and to dream about the person I wanted to be, someone just like them.

And there she was, one of the most important people in my life at that time, making me laugh and forget that I was in a psychiatric ward. Her being there told me that I was more to her than a job, and that she really did care about me. For a fifteen year old kid who wanted to die, it meant more than she would ever know. I didn't need a tutor, but I did need a friend, and she was there when I needed her most.

Miss A was the teacher who told me I was going to be admitted to the hospital, the teacher who held me when I was in the school nurse's office suffering from a breakdown, and the teacher who walked out in the middle of a class and came running down the hall when she got word that I was in trouble. That day was particularly horrible.

A group of girls convinced me that we were going to skip class. We detoured into the industrial arts building which in hindsight should have raised my suspicion. Once we were in a back office behind the empty classroom, they shut and blocked the door. One girl announced that they were staging an intervention, and told me that the police had been called. They also informed me that I wasn't going anywhere until I got help. As I tried to escape, someone attempted to physically restrain me and my best friend Theresa jumped to my defense, pinning her against the wall and threatening her never to lay hands on me again. I don't know how long we were in that room, but fortunately the teacher to whom the classroom belonged eventually came to the rescue. The girls were reprimanded and sent back to class, while I was escorted to the office with police officers in tow. Theresa ran down the hall and banged on Miss A's door yelling to her that I was in trouble. Despite having a classroom full of gawking students, Miss A left them all behind and came to be with me, helping me navigate through what transpired next.

She was not only there when I was in crisis, but also convinced a boy I liked to dance with me at the school dance, adopted one of my cat's kittens, and was now volunteering as a tutor so she could sneak into a hospital ward to visit me and make me laugh at one of the lowest points in my life. Whether my adoration of her was considered unhealthy or not, I still believe it was fully warranted, as she was an amazing human being.

Throughout my journey, the love and compassion shown to me by many of the teachers and staff at both Shaw Junior High and at Gorham High School was incredible. From the Spanish teacher who was gifted in her ability to make me laugh and smile, the art teacher who served as a silent role model, or the school nurse who let me sit in her office whenever I was having a bad day, they all touched me in different ways. I will also never forget the guidance counselor who made it a point to check in and one day presented me with a rosebud pendant necklace that she said represented who I was now, but that someday I would make it and become a rose. This act of kindness, as well as countless others over the years, made all the difference in the world to me, a child who was lost and wanted to die, but who found love and support from teachers and staff who every day did so much more than what was expected of them.

Journal Entry – April 19, 1989

I was thinking this afternoon about how I seem to always stop talking in mid-sentence and was wondering what some of the reasons for that might be. It's been something I've done for as long as I can remember and at times people have confronted me about it and I've never been real sure of an answer. When I start talking to people I'll start out alright (usually) but as I say things my mind drifts and I remove myself from whatever it is I'm saying. I feel like it's not really me speaking and I'm not aware of what I'm saying. I think that may have something to do with all the contradicting ideas that the nurses picked up on. I wasn't always aware of exactly what it was that I was saying. Does that make any sense? My mind would start racing – some of it would come out in half sentences and the rest would just drift. I don't know if the drifting is just losing touch with my thoughts or what. One thing I think both you and the hospital have done for me over the past several weeks is made me aware of different things about myself. I'll see you in 39 ½ hours (2370 minutes)!

Ami DeRienzo

CHAPTER 13

If you saw the movie *Girl Interrupted* starring Wynona Ryder and Angelina Jolie, it might help you to understand me a little better. Sadly, I am nowhere near as good looking as either of them, but my psychiatrist and other mental health professionals seemed to agree that Wynona's character and I shared a diagnosis. As much as I'd love to be able to identify with the more exciting, thrill seeking Angelina Jolie role, that wasn't me. I did fall in love with a few characters much like her over the years, but I will spare them the indignity of discussing their mental health in this public manner. Suffice it to say, they were equally as charming and charismatic as Angelina, and putting our craziness together created quite an adventure. Chances are good that if you did see the movie, you likely won't remember much about either of their conditions unless you are a mental health professional yourself or could relate to the characters in the way that I could. I'm not going to rehash the movie, but figured I would give you a point of reference for the diagnosis that was given me. It is a good movie, and quite an accurate depiction of what a psychiatric ward in the eighties was like.

After many tests that came back with a mixed bag of results ranging from delusional to genius, psychotic to other, they finally found a label that seemed to stick, and I received an official diagnosis when I was in my early teens. Before I make the great reveal, I just need to backtrack here for a second. Not that I'm paranoid or anything, but I don't want anyone reading that last sentence to wonder if I am indeed psychotic. What was happening was that I was being given many complex psychiatric tests that would present questions that I found to be vague. For instance, "Do you hear voices?" Now perhaps some people would read that question, and the answer would be a simple yes or no. That is not how my brain works.... When I am asked this question, I immediately go into philosophical/analytical mode. When there are people talking around me, I hear voices. Sometimes I sense an inner voice telling me something is right or wrong which may not be audible in the classic sense, but I can hear it nonetheless. Sometimes I think I may hear someone say my name, and then I turn around and there's no one there. Do you see my dilemma? As a forty something year old, I know now what they are asking despite the fact that my brain is still wired to overanalyze everything and wants to dissect the question and discover its hidden meaning, but as a young kid? I agonized over every question. I was raised Baptist, so I naturally had to go with the honest answer and say yes... Am I psychotic? I don't think so... Most likely, I was simply too analytical, philosophical, literal, and guilt-ridden to test properly.

My nickname growing up was Amelia Bedelia, a children's book character I adored and could relate to on so many levels. When Amelia was instructed to "dress the turkey," she would literally put the turkey in a dress. That was how I rolled. When my test results first came back saying I was psychotic, I think this shook my therapist up a bit, but she quickly came to my defense and said it wasn't true, knowing me well enough to be able to confidently assert that I couldn't possibly be psychotic.

More than anything, I was just bad at all things subjective, and the art of decision making involved in test taking would haunt me as an Achilles heel throughout my entire life. In my management career, these decision making challenges were a constant reality. An associate might approach me and ask, "Miss DeRienzo, should we stock the truck or do price changes first?" If they could only see what was taking place in my head during that thirty second delay from when the question was asked and answered, they probably would have opted to figure it out on their own. My brain would immediately go into spreadsheet/graph mode where I would analyze the data, the pros and cons that would come with each possible scenario and the projected end result. It's like having a computer instead of a mind, except that this computer was designed in the early seventies and still takes floppy disks. Eventually I'll get there, but it takes me a little longer to process the information. While some interpreted my pauses over the years as indecision, the reality was that I was simply experiencing information overload and a desire to achieve the perfect outcome. I suppose I could have made quick decisions if I wanted to, but I was much more interested in trying to achieve perfection.

Given the complex way in which my brain seems to work, it was hard for them to get an accurate diagnosis, but eventually they settled on something called Borderline Personality Disorder with additional disassociation and splitting. I'd never heard of it until that day when it became my official label, but I did my research after the fact and accepted that it was likely an accurate assessment. Looking back now, I think how much easier it would have been to have had the internet in those days. I could have Googled it instead of spending all those hours in the library, but alas… If I had the luxury of search engine results, I might have suggested to them that it is possible I may have a touch of OCD and an anxiety disorder as well, although I don't remember it being quite so bad in my younger years as it seems to be today.

While I realize you likely have your smart phone within arm's reach, and perhaps you are even reading this on your phone, I will spare you the trouble of having to Google. Borderline Personality Disorder is what caused Wynona's character to slit her wrists and to behave badly. It became an official diagnosis back in 1980 which is likely why we had never heard of it since I received my diagnosis just a few years later. I imagine everyone's experience is different and because of this, I will stick to how BPD was affecting my life at the time, and maybe the real life illustrations will be easier to understand than the text book explanation.

One way my diagnosis showed itself was that I could be extreme on the emotional swing. I had a tendency to see the world as a place made up of many heroes and villains. If you were someone I identified as one of the heroes, I adored you and thought you walked on water. I couldn't see your faults or your humanity. You were a goddess who I would follow to the ends of the earth. If you hurt me or shattered my illusion of who I thought you were, my world would fall apart. In those days, if one of these people expressed the slightest bit of criticism or disappointment, there would be a quick downward spiral that ultimately resulted in self-destructive behavior. For instance, I would be sitting in a classroom and a teacher I liked would pass back a paper that had the slightest bit of criticism, something silly like "You used there instead of their," and it would send me spiraling. It wasn't that my view of the teacher would crash, but I would be completely devastated that I had failed them as was apparent through their criticism. My BPD brain would tell me that I deserved to be punished for my failure. I would ask for a pass, go down the hall to the bathroom, and cut myself with a straight edge razor blade. Then I would wrap my arm in toilet paper to prevent the blood from seeping through, pull down my sleeve, and return back to class. I would have to draw blood or it wouldn't count. It was the only way I could keep going when I knew that I had done something wrong that had disappointed someone I cared about.

If you were a villain, and by this I mean that when I met you my first impression was that you were cold, demanding, loud, superficial, angry, or gruff, there really wasn't much you could do to convince me otherwise. I had no room in my world for people like you. If I heard you raise your voice in anger, if your eyes were not soft and your tone not gentle, there is a good chance you would have fallen into this category. Though I may have someday let you graduate to the level of neutral, you would never be one of the heroes, and I would always approach you with wary caution.

There are of course many who would fall into the neutral category including all those people who I never let get close enough to do me harm. It was the heroes and the villains, however, who I had to be cautious of. One of the biggest issues that people with BPD face is their inability to have healthy relationships which has a lot to do with the extreme emotions of loving someone quickly and intensely, and then experiencing the crash when another's humanity causes them to ultimately fail to live up to the idealistic expectations put upon them. With BPD, there also comes mood swings and impulsiveness which can be rough, especially in an intimate or family type of relationship. Like those battling manic-depression, it can be fun when you are chasing after the latest love of your life, but when reality comes crashing in, it can cause extreme feelings of sadness and depression. Being bad at relationships applied to more than just romance, and unfortunately affected me in a number of different ways over the years.

Self-destructive behavior is but another aspect of BPD that was quite relevant in my case. They say the tendency toward self-destructive behavior presents itself in a variety of ways, and unfortunately for my poor mom and dad, I explored just about all of them during my teenage years. While my illness affected the way in which I was able to relate to people in my life, being an overly sensitive child who didn't know how to process some significant life events also contributed to my inability to function in a traditional manner.

One of the final identifying characteristics that I exhibited that is common in folks with borderline personality disorder is that I could be extremely impulsive. The way this would often play out is that I would get some "great idea" in my head and would have to immediately follow through. When you're a kid, being impulsive generally doesn't get noticed quite as much as when you are an adult and do crazy things like send flowers to a complete stranger at the doctor's office because she was kind to you or to show up at a friend's workplace after hearing that her mom was in the hospital and trying to buy her a week's vacation in order to allow her to spend time with her mom. I imagine sometimes people likely thought I was creepy given my impulsive nature and lack of appropriate boundaries in certain circumstances, especially when I entered the bar scene later in life. Lucky for me, however, this is exactly the type of behavior that led me to find my life partner. After seeing her run out of the bar crying one night, I acted on my impulse to follow her to make sure she was okay. Fifteen years later... I guess that was one impulsive act that ended up with a happy ending, and thankfully she was not carrying pepper spray!

Journal Entry – 4/16/1989

I think the reason I was so scared to go home was partly out of fear of losing you. I used to look forward to each new day because I knew I'd see you. Each weekend I told myself, "Monday Morning! You can make it 'til then!" I grow to depend on people so much and love them so much that they pull away. I'm aware that I do it, but I don't know how to stop. Other than totally isolating myself and shutting off my feelings, how can I stop loving so much?

It's funny. I know next to nothing about you, you know, your life after the role of playing doctor all day. And yet, I feel as though I couldn't live without you. I'm always so scared that something's going to happen to you. If you came in to the hospital later than usual, I'd go nuts with worry thinking that maybe something had happened and you were hurt somewhere or even dead. The reason I ask you so many personal questions all the time is my way of checking out the situation and making sure you are safe. I don't mean to pry into your personal life with my questions, but I need to know that nothing's going to happen to you. If I was capable of hurting you, I'd give you up to protect you. I don't want to ever hurt you or anybody.

CHAPTER 14

"Please, Mom! We just want to go the mall for a couple hours. The other kids do it all the time!"

My poor mother finally caved. I was such a handful, and at that point in my life there wasn't much that I got excited about. A new friend from school who I may have had a slight crush on had asked me to come spend the day with her. While my mom likely assumed two girls going to the mall meant a desire to shop, it had nothing to do with that. I was not, am not, will never be the type of girl you will find shopping at the mall. We were going to meet some guys that my friend knew through her older brothers, but there is no way we were going to share that little piece of information with my mother. Not knowing any better, Mom agreed to take us to the mall where she would give us free reign for one hour while she did some shopping. We decided upon a meeting place, and took off as quickly as we could.

He had long black hair that went down to his waist, more earrings than I could count without being obvious about what I was doing, and eye lashes that were so dark I figured and then later confirmed was indeed mascara. He and the other guys looked like they belonged in an eighties rock band, ripped spandex and all. While the rest of the guys were all gushing over my friend, this one had his eyes on me, and I couldn't believe it. In those days, if a guy came up to you and told you that you had nice boobs, you took that as a compliment and not sexual harassment. At least when you were an attention starved seventh grade girl with self-esteem issues, you thought it was the equivalent of being told you were special. I had never been the object of someone's affection and did not know quite what to do with it. Within the hour, I was making out with this older guy who I had just met. I was about twelve, and he was sixteen. Of course my friend and I both looked older and tried to present ourselves as far more experienced than we were, working hard to impress the guys.

His name was Bobby, and we were still lip locked when my mother came to tear me away. Horrified would probably be a good word to describe her reaction. At the same time, she had no way of knowing what an added stressor he would become in their lives for several years to follow, or she definitely would have been horrified. I don't know if the stories Bobby told me were true, but he confessed to having quite a sordid past in which his father had killed his mother and then committed suicide. He informed me that he had recently gotten out of juvenile detention after serving time for manslaughter, and had lived on the streets for most of his life battling drug addiction. Being a young girl, I found all this to be romantic and exciting, convinced that perhaps I could give him the love he had never known and that I could somehow save him like I had tried to save that bird. He wrote me poetry and long love letters. He even stole a gold heart necklace that he gave me to think of him when he wasn't around. I ate it all up, convinced that we would be together, and I would be the one who would help him to heal after his lifetime of hurt.

Despite my parents' efforts to keep us apart, the more they tried, the harder I pushed back determined to make my own decisions no matter how reckless they were. One day I even went so far as to run away with him. Fortunately, in hindsight, he didn't have a car, so we only got as far as we could go on foot, which under the circumstances was still quite impressive. We walked from Gorham all the way to the mall in South Portland where we had first met, a good nine mile hike. I still don't know how they ever found us, but my parents pulled up to the street corner where we were waiting for one of his buddies to pick us up, ordering me into the car. From that day on, they did whatever they could to keep me away from him. What finally did the trick, however, was when he got thrown back into prison. For years, he continued to write, begging me to wait for him, until one day the letters just stopped. It wasn't until much later in high school after my hospitalization that I realized that my parents had been intercepting his letters and hiding them from me. I was devastated to learn that he thought I had abandoned him, when in fact I thought he had abandoned me.

After about twenty-five years of not hearing anything else from Bobby or being able to track him down as he must have gotten transferred to a new prison facility, I was reading the local paper one day and saw that he had been killed in what looked like a drug deal gone bad. Though I know it was hard for my parents to do what they did in applying that tough love, I am certain that it played a role in my survival as a young person. Though I was absolutely furious at the time when I found out they had intercepted my mail, it is obvious to me now that I was too vulnerable, a prime candidate to have fallen into a life of drug addiction and abuse had they not intervened. Though I had resented them for doing so, their tough stance had truly been an act of love that ultimately saved me from myself.

This had been the first of many unhealthy relationships that would follow and consume my teen years of impulsive living and poor decision making. The word no didn't seem to be in my vocabulary unless it was directed at an authority figure, and it was as if I had a sign on my forehead giving predators an open invitation to come and enter my life. Given the difficulty I had relating to my peers, it was often older guys that came along and gave me the attention I craved. At school I was still socially awkward and had a difficult time with relationships, especially with boys my own age. Some of the guys at my school could be downright mean. While I've often heard that girls are more horrible to each other than guys, in my experience I found my female classmates to be much kinder. They didn't make fun of me like the guys did, at least not to my face.

In an effort to keep me pure (my poor parents), I was not allowed to actually go out on a date until I turned sixteen. Of course I had found many ways around this in my early teens, but still looked forward to the day when I would be allowed to walk out the front door instead of having to climb out the window. Though I had been released from the hospital by the time I was old enough to date, I was still considered an outpatient and would go there at least a couple times a week for therapy. On one such occasion, I was approached by a mid-eastern man who was mopping the floors. Though I can't remember his exact line, it was something like, "You very pretty. Maybe me take you out sometime? Me have your number?" Of course I was thrilled that someone thought I was worth approaching. I could have cared less that he was a janitor and not a doctor. Those things never mattered to me.

As my mother groaned, I pulled out a pen and paper and gave him my number. I had just turned sixteen and was excited to be able to go out on my first official date. He pulled up in front of the house and waited for me to come out which should have been the first warning sign. I was just a dumb kid who didn't know any better, I guess.

He took me to what I thought was a nice restaurant in Old Orchard Beach, but it really could have been anywhere for all I know. I had quite low expectations as to what constituted a nice restaurant back in those days. At the time we met, I was in the midst of my anorexic phase, another coping mechanism I adopted to replace the cutting after leaving the hospital. When it came time to order, I stated that all I wanted was a salad. In response to this, he became angry and insisted that I had insulted him by not ordering food. I didn't know at the time if his reaction was a cultural thing or if he was worried that I wouldn't put out if he didn't spend enough money on me. Despite how uncomfortable he made me feel, I wasn't about to put food into my body. I picked at the salad when it came, moving it around my plate trying to make it look like I had eaten something.

After leaving the restaurant, we went into a few shops where he insisted on buying me a gift which I refused to accept for fear that it would be interpreted as me owing him something. Seriously, what would I do with a $30.00 bedazzled handbag from Old Orchard Beach anyway? Good grief...

Our date was obviously not going well, and as the night went on, he became more and more agitated. When we got into the car, he attempted to get physical, and I asked him to bring me home. By showing me his short temper, he had landed himself in the villain category, and I really wanted to have nothing to do with him. As we drove, he asked about seeing me again, to which I replied that I didn't think it was a good idea. He pulled over, and I was immediately frightened. Then he started to hit himself in the head and cry, apologizing for his behavior. He told me about his childhood and how he had watched as his family was murdered and how he had been forced to flee to the States during the civil war in his home country. The caretaker in me took over, and I couldn't suppress the feelings of empathy. As soon as I agreed to see him again, his tears suddenly vanished, and we were on our way.

It was that second time that it happened. Because of the behavior I'd observed on our first date, I was cautious and even a little afraid of being alone with him again. Normally I may have trusted my gut instinct, but my feelings of sympathy for his experience and that ability to picture him as a little boy enduring such horrible suffering overrode my better judgment. We went out, and this time the sexual advances throughout the evening were aggressive and intense, to the point where I just wanted the night to end and to never see this guy again. When I suggested it was time to go home, he was not happy as we got into the car. After driving a short distance, he turned down a dimly lit road and then off into an empty church parking lot. He opened his door and walked around to my side of the vehicle. It seemed to happen in such a way that it was surreal. All I could think was that this can't possibly be happening. Then he raped me, brutally and without remorse, all the while saying, *"You like it! You like it!"* while I cried and begged him to stop.

While Bobby may have been considered by some to be a hoodlum and I guess he was, he had never been anything but gentle and kind. This man, on the other hand, was a monster. When he was done, he drove me home in silence. I walked in the door, my knees bloody and mascara running down my face. I was too ashamed to tell anyone what had happened, though I eventually confided in my therapist and my big sister. Being that he worked at the hospital where my therapist was employed, I would not be surprised if she were responsible for the fact that I never saw him again when I went there for therapy.

My sister Beth ran into him once some time later at the mall and told me that she went up to him and smacked him across the face. I cannot express the love I felt for her when she told me that, or how proud I am even today that she came to my defense in that way. If you know my sister, she is an introvert, so decking people at least physically is not something that one would expect from her. It was the most loving thing any big sister could have done, and it meant the world to me. She says now, some thirty years later, that she can't remember this ever happening, although I can recall clearly the day she told me about it. My sister had a tendency to make things up sometimes that simply weren't true, especially when talking with her little sister, and her guess is that this may have been one of those times. However, real or not, the fact that she told me she did it was her way of saying that she was not okay with what happened to me. She was telling me that it wasn't my fault and that I deserved to be protected. She was telling me in her own way that despite our constant sibling rivalry and bickering, that she was there and loved me even if she couldn't say the words. Because of this, it doesn't matter to me if she embellished the truth or completely made up that story. It was the love behind it that meant the world to me and not the slap whether real or embellished.

Just as I had one day read about Bobby's sad ending in the local paper, the monster who raped me also had a news story. Unfortunately, however, it was not about him receiving justice, but detailed the suffering of one of his victims. The article told of how he had bought a fifteen year old girl from her mother, which I am guessing may have been to support a drug habit. The mother gave him her daughter with her permission to marry, and with the laws being as messed up as they are, a judge allowed it to happen despite the fact that he was twenty-nine years old at the time. The news story broke revealing that he had brutalized this poor girl continuously throughout their short marriage, and he was eventually arrested after putting her in the hospital.

While he was awaiting trial, I went down to the police station and told them my story. More than anything, I just wanted them to know what a dangerous man they had on their hands if there had been any doubt in their minds. They had no doubts, however, and they said that more than ten other girls had come forward with similar stories since his arrest. Hearing this made me feel even more guilt than I felt when initially reading about his child bride. I wondered if these girls had been hurt before or after I had, and if there was some way that I could have saved them had I been stronger and come forward.

It was a different time back then. Since I had agreed to go out on a date with him, it felt like it somehow wasn't the same as real rape, like perhaps it was my fault for going out with him in the first place or for making him angry. But had I known, had I been able to see what a predator he was and that it wasn't my fault, perhaps I could have raised an alarm about his character or found a way to warn the others. Unfortunately, justice was never served. Whether through intimidation or just the brokenness of our court system, he received less than a slap on the wrist and was back on the streets, living the American dream. While this man happened to be a refugee and a Muslim, this is not what made him a monster. While I imagine his childhood trauma may have played a role in creating him, there are many men I have known who have experienced similar horrors who would never come close to doing anything as evil as this man was guilty of. Whatever it was that tainted him or whether he was just born to be something without a conscience, I will never know.

Over the years I grew to understand that there are people on this planet who may have crazy outfits, long hair, and tattoos but are the sweetest and most gentle souls you will ever know. Others may hide behind a gruff exterior, talk loud, and may even swear up a storm, but when you take the time to get to know them, there is so much more to them than what they show on the surface. At the same time, I also learned that an attractive, smooth talking, seemingly sentimental and sympathetic exterior can harbor the most dangerous of monsters. Perhaps some people learn this earlier in life than I did, maybe because I had a BPD brain and wasn't always the greatest at deciphering superheroes from villains, or having the ability to see anyone as an integrated human being with both strengths and weaknesses. I eventually learned, however, that heroes and villains don't always come in the type of package you expect them to. In the same way, love doesn't always look the way we think it should either.

CHAPTER 15

"Ami, what are you feeling right now?"

As usual, I looked down at my hands, around the room and down at the floor, anything to avoid her question. The arms of the chair were starting to show a worn indentation from where I would anxiously pick at the wood during our sessions. I couldn't look at her, couldn't explain or express the emptiness that seemed to engulf me. I didn't feel anything that I could associate with anything else. It was just dark nothingness. We sat in awkward silence, something we stumbled upon frequently. How could I tell her that the only thought I could focus on was that in thirty-seven minutes our session would be over, and she would be gone? How could I possibly explain the panic and anxiety that came from knowing that I would now have to wait another forty-eight hours and thirty-seven minutes before I would see her again and that I didn't know if I could make it? When I was there with her, I could find a reason to stay, to continue life on this planet, but in those times in between... It was so hard...

"I'm wondering what your life is like outside of here..."

"Okay, but that's a thought, not a feeling. I was asking what you are feeling right now... Can you tell me?"

Pivot, distract, dodge, run... These were essential tools to survive therapy. I didn't want to talk about feelings, and I didn't want to talk about me. I wanted to know everything about her, what she loved and what she dreamed of. Over a span of about ten years, I was able to pry little tidbits here and there to try to unravel the mystery of Dr. White. It makes me laugh now, as I think of the "quid pro quo" line from the *Silence of the Lambs* movie. I tried this on her many a time, the old "you show me yours and I'll show you mine" trick, the barter system being applied to psychotherapy. Occasionally it worked, and I was able to squeeze a little out of her. Most of the time, she just waited me out, or decided to go in the back door. Sometimes that meant we talked about baby birds feeling abandoned or shamed, or perhaps falling to their death or being murdered. Sometimes we would just go for a walk or play a game. It generally didn't matter much to me what we did, as long as I was with her I felt safe.

I first ended up in Dr. White's office after the controversial yet well-intentioned intervention that my peers managed to pull off. In the years prior to that event, the school had gotten involved in seeking mental health care for me and encouraged my parents to do the same. Up until that point, however, interactions I had were limited primarily to the school nurse, guidance counselor, and social worker. In an effort to appease the school, my parents sent me to a religious male counselor who quite frankly gave me the creeps. I didn't feel comfortable or safe with him, and it was quite horrific. He insisted on dragging in all my little brothers and sisters for family sessions, and I think we were all a little traumatized. Thankfully, that venture didn't last long.

By my freshman year, however, things were spiraling out of control. I was placed in an alternative education program which basically helped me be able to cut class and smoke at school without getting suspended. Since my issues were not of an academic nature, it was difficult to find a place for me that made any sense. I was a college prep kid for most of the day and in an alternative education program for study hall. This allowed me to receive special mental health services and accommodations through the school.

The intervention had been orchestrated by a girl who hung out with some of my friends and had caught wind of the rumors that must have been going around at school about me. This act of someone who hardly knew me resulted in my parents being formally threatened with the possibility that they could lose custody of me if I did not receive professional help, since her call to the police had in turn prompted a call to DHS. This is how I ended up getting officially evaluated, tested, and diagnosed. It is also how I ended up seeing child psychiatrist Dr. White twice a week until I was ultimately hospitalized at the age of fifteen.

As scary as it was to be admitted, the benefit of hospitalization was that instead of having sessions a couple times a week, I would get to see Dr. White at least once a day with the exception of the weekends. Though sometimes it was just a five minute check in to see how I was doing, I knew she was always close by and could occasionally catch a glimpse of her out the hospital window as she walked across the parking lot. She was my greatest advocate, the highlight of my day, my friend, sister, mother, and caregiver all rolled into one.

While the hospital was not at all how I imagined it would be, it also was not what many might think of when they hear the words insane asylum or mental hospital either. There was an occasional straight jacket that would be pulled out in extreme situations where a resident posed a threat to themselves or to someone else, but overall this was not the norm. Being that I was placed in a psychiatric ward within a traditional hospital, the patients tended to be folks who were there as a form of crisis intervention or temporary holding. Those who needed long-term or permanent care were typically sent off to a group home or residential facility after they were properly stabilized. Because of this, the ward contained an extremely diverse group of individuals in crisis. There was a mom struggling with post-partum depression, and others who had lost the will to live due to the death of a loved one. There were young people with anger issues and destructive tendencies, and an older man with obvious dementia who was receiving shock treatments. Everyone was battling their own demons, from paranoid schizophrenics to young kids with phobias and eating disorders. Perhaps the saddest of all were those who were there because they had no place to go, elderly folks with no home or family to speak of. One of my senior roommates confided in me that this was her reason for being there. For her, the hospital was the only place in the world where she felt she belonged. We were her family.

As the weeks went by, I made many friends in the hospital, and they became a surrogate family for me as well. We attended group sessions, participated in activities and an occasional outing, had meals together in the day room, and shared a kitchen where I found joy making cookies for the other residents. One of my best memories was of an elderly woman on the ward who refused to get out of bed. The nurses all insisted that there was nothing wrong with her physically, although she pretended that she couldn't walk. The nurses felt that it was because she did not want to socialize with us. In order to get her out of her room, they would have to put her in a wheelchair and bring her to out for dinner kicking and screaming. When anyone would go near her, she would yell profanities at them and insist they go away. Always up for a challenge, I decided I would try to break through to this woman and find a way to engage. Though she was gruff, for some reason I didn't see her as one of the bad guys.

With a plate full of freshly baked chocolate chip cookies, I made my way down to her room. She eyed me suspiciously, until it was obvious that she realized I was carrying something of potential interest. While she didn't yell at me which was a win all by itself, she was still far from friendly, waving her hand at me and telling me to get out. I smiled and told her that I would place the cookies right over there on the counter on the other side of the room, in case she changed her mind.

One of the nurses was in on my little social experiment, and waited for me out in the hallway to see how it went. I had closed the door behind me but left it open just enough that we could watch her. As soon as she thought I was gone, this woman jumped up like a five year old on Christmas morning and grabbed the plate of cookies, running back to bed with them. The nurse and I shared a grin, and then left her to eat her cookies in private. From that day on, the woman seemed to have a bit of an attitude adjustment and started to join the rest of us for meals in the day room. While she never transformed into a social butterfly and maintained a gruff exterior when people got too close, she and I seemed to have a special connection for the remainder of our time together in hospital.

Being at the hospital felt safe, and after getting used to the loss of freedom, it was actually a relief not to have to make any major decisions. It was like becoming a child again for all of us, learning to trust our caregivers and to depend on them to keep us safe. As with any family, there were times when things got rough, when someone would have a bad day and would get hauled off to isolation, or even worse be taken to AMHI, the mental institution we all feared being banished to. There were other days when we would have to say goodbye to someone who didn't want to leave and that was also hard. There were many good days too, though, where we just had fun in a world where we could be who we were without judgment.

One thing that has always been important to me even in my darkest times was maintaining a sense of humor. For us crazy folks, there was nothing more fun than messing with the heads of the "normal" people who would come to visit the ward or who were there to drop off family members in need of treatment. Perhaps it was a little cruel, but when we saw the look of terror on their faces as they came off the elevator, knowing that their fear was based on what they'd seen in a horror movie, it was just too much fun not to exploit. It made me wonder if the girl dancing in the hallway when I first arrived was the same joke being played on me and my parents.

It was around Easter time, and one way in which we decided to have fun was to roll plastic Easter eggs into the elevator doors when people would come and go through the locked entrance. Though the timing of it could make it a little tricky, getting the egg in before the elevator doors closed, it was something to pass the time. We wrote little messages inside the eggs, such as "Help me! I'm a prisoner being held on the 6th floor!" While we were a small band of adolescents in a heavily adult populated ward, we still found a way to be delinquent teenagers.

Journal Entry – 4/23/1989
(8 Days after Release from Hospital)

I feel so lonely and scared. I've felt so empty lately. Nothing's really happened. I don't have any reason for feeling so low, no excuse, I just do. It seems like all I ever think about it dying. The only times I ever feel safe is when I'm with you or if someone is holding me. That sucks because I don't have anyone who will hold me, so I count down the minutes until I am with you again and feel safe. The hospital helped me a lot but it stirred up so many feelings and emotions in me that I just can't deal with without being destroyed. I'm so scared and confused. I feel like I've lost all motivation to do anything. It all seems meaningless and I just don't care anymore. It seems like a never ending battle. I could try and work for years and then kill myself. I know someday I will, and I just don't see the importance of preparing for the future. I'm not going to have a future.

It scared me when you said you could go to jail if I committed suicide as an out-patient. I told you before I'd never do anything to hurt you in any way, and I meant it. While I'm under your care, the only way I'd possibly die is by accident. I'd do anything, even live, to protect you...

CHAPTER 16

"Ami, we have something to tell you..."

I wasn't ready for that day. It came so suddenly that there was no time to prepare, much like when I had arrived. The nurse informed me that my family's insurance had run out and that I was to be sent home the next day. I had been living on the ward for a month during which time I had little connection or exposure to the outside world. It was like existing in an alternate reality protected by a bubble, where I didn't have to deal with the everyday stresses of high school and boys and fighting with my parents. I had come to accept this place as my home, full of new friends and staff that had become a part of my life. The thought of leaving overwhelmed and terrified me. I didn't want to go. I wanted to stay here forever. I wasn't ready and could not deal with the thought of being thrust back into the chaos that had been my life prior to the hospital.

The decision had been made and there was no going back. The insurance company had spoken, and it was what it was. My hospital bills already exceeded a quarter of a million dollars which back in the eighties was even more of a ridiculous amount of money than it is today. There was just no way. The financial burden my parents were carrying was already far beyond their ability to manage. Without the insurance company, the only option for residential treatment would be if I became a ward of the state, and that was an option no one was willing to consider.

After leaving the hospital under such turbulent conditions, I quickly resorted back to my old ways after going home, and the threats began again. If I did not stop cutting, the state would have no choice but to step in, and I would be placed in permanent residential treatment where I would likely be held until I turned eighteen. This was not something I wanted to see happen, mostly out of fear that I would lose control and be separated from Dr. White. I learned other ways to cope and release the crazy that I was feeling inside, ways that were not as obvious as the scars on my body. From drugs and alcohol, sexual promiscuity to self-starvation, if there was a way to hurt myself without getting caught, I would find the means to do it. I started skipping school and doing what I could to hold on and not disappear.

Being back in the real world meant learning how to live again, putting back on the protective layer that had been methodically stripped away while I was in the hospital. It meant rebuilding the wall and finding new means of self-preservation. I did what I had to do. While on the surface I was presenting as a conformist, in reality I had just adapted to the situation and learned how to take care of myself. After leaving the hospital, I stopped eating and with my 5"6 height, my weight dropped from about one hundred and ten down to eighty-eight in the course of several months. I would carefully count and control every calorie that entered my body and the less I ate, the more my stomach seemed to shrink until I no longer had the ability to feel hunger.

Having worked at a restaurant throughout high school, one of our perks was free food. In my case, my employers made out quite well during this time period. Each day the cook would humor me by creating a saltine sandwich which consisted of a single cracker, about a teaspoon or was it half a teaspoon of whipped cream with a maraschino cherry on top. Yes, I was a little quirky, and if I remember right, this favorite meal of mine was twenty-seven calories. I also had a pet plastic dinosaur that came with me wherever I went. My Spanish teacher affectionately named him Fugly because according to her, he was so "F-ing ugly!" This was one thing teachers apparently could get away with back then without fear of reprimand, actually connecting on a human level with their students whether that meant giving them a hug or having conversations with their plastic dinosaurs. Fugly would sit on the corner of my desk in class, as I would carve skulls and gravestones with a jackknife into my notebooks and book covers, another activity that I'm sure is frowned upon today.

While my efforts at self-starvation went unnoticed for a period of time, eventually my weight loss became alarming enough to raise concerns. The possibility of hospitalization was once again put on the table, only this time it would be a different facility. Though I would have happily gone back to the hospital where my beloved Dr. White was, I had no intention of being placed somewhere that would prevent her from being able to be my therapist.

One night around this time when I was at a particular low point, I happened to turn on the television and saw a woman appealing to anyone who may be hurting or who had lost hope. I could tell by listening to her and looking in her eyes that she was one of the good people. She was kind and compassionate, someone who seemed to genuinely believe the words that she was saying and who wanted to help. She was telling me not to give up, that there was hope, and that there was a God who loved me just the way I am. Her message was one of acceptance and unconditional love as she spoke of a God who wasn't looking for the perfect candidate to do His bidding, but rather sought to heal my wounds through compassion and love, that I didn't have to be "good enough," and that I was precious in His eyes.

I felt so broken and lost and to hear a stranger offering hope, any hope, it was a freeing experience. For most of my life God had been an angry figure casting judgment upon who I was and everything that I had done. He had taken away my grandfather, allowed that baby bird to be abandoned and die, and had caused me to be born a misfit. Now here this lady was, telling me that everything that I thought about God was wrong, that God loved me the way I was and that He offers comfort and peace, not stress and heavy expectations. Of course I had heard the "God is love" message throughout my life, but hearing it and believing it are two entirely different things. To me, God had always been someone to fear, someone who I would never be good enough for, and who couldn't possibly love me with all my evil thoughts. This woman, however, in that moment when I needed her most, managed to get through to me in a way endless hours of sitting through church never had. It was like a thousand years of sorrow spilled out of me and I wept. I had tried everything else… Why not God?

CHAPTER 17

There was a line waiting to talk with me, to shake my hand, and to tell me the ways in which they too had been hurt. It was mostly young, teenage girls from broken homes who had been the victims of some type of physical or sexual abuse, kids who at one point or another also wanted to die. This was not my first speaking engagement, but it was perhaps my biggest. The lights in the auditorium had been dimmed, and there I was center stage in the spotlight with microphone in hand, telling my story. It was surreal and a bit overwhelming to think that I might possibly have something to offer all these kids who were looking to me for hope.

Like everything in my life, when I shifted my focus, I became all in. Following my spiritual awakening that night when I was watching TV, I came to the conclusion that my mission in life was now to reach out to others and to try to offer that same hope that was offered to me. The hope that maybe life was about more than what we could see and feel right now, that perhaps the darkness was just a tunnel, one from which we would eventually pass through and come out into the light on the other side. I wanted to reach out to other kids like me who believed the only way to find acceptance was through achieving perfection and that atonement demanded self-inflicted punishment. I wanted kids to know that they really were good enough, just the way they were, and that they didn't have to feel the shame or the guilt that I did. That it didn't matter how many times they may have screwed up, that they were precious both in my eyes and in the eyes of God.

I was invited to speak at youth groups, church events, and even a private high school, before finding myself here in a stadium with hundreds of eyes upon me. That constant hunger I felt throughout my life had finally found a positive means of fulfillment that came with the joy of helping others. At the time, I had put together a very rough and elementary booklet that consisted of journal entries from throughout my teenage years including my time in the hospital. As these booklets circulated, I began receiving letters from teens reaching out to me as if I had the answers, with some letters even coming from juvenile detention facilities as far away as Texas. For the first time in my life, I felt needed, like there was finally something I held that was of value to someone, something I could give back.

Things happened quickly. I went from being a self-starving anorexic to a teenage writer and guest speaker overnight. Not only did my spiritual conversion result in church related activities, but I also became involved in politics on issues such as abortion and gay rights. My brother and I stood together in pro-life picket lines and attended local Right to Life meetings. At this time, the city of Portland was also considering enactment of its first gay rights ordinance, and my brother was working closely with the woman who led the opposition to the bill. Reflecting back on my involvement in this now makes me cringe with regret and sadness, especially since many who were fighting on the other side became my dearest friends and surrogate family in the years that followed. Regardless, having these experiences did teach me a lot about perspective, and how quickly that can change when faced with someone else's or even your own reality.

As for my role in our political activism, I was busy challenging the school curriculum at my local high school, the school where the teachers and staff had cared for me throughout my turbulent years and were now suddenly forming an alliance as the opposition party. It all began when I was sitting in one of my favorite classes and was handed an assignment that was called "Questions for Exploring Your Sexual Orientation." We were told that we must answer the questions asked and then turn them in for a grade. I was horrified, and still remember those questions almost thirty years later. They included asking specifically when I had chosen my sexual orientation, and how difficult would it be for me to change. It then went on to state things such as the majority of child molesters are straight, and then asked why straight people are so sexually aggressive... There was more, but you get the idea...

The intent of the assignment was really to make us think about the stereotypes that exist around homosexuality and essentially point out that these stereotypes are all wrong. In today's society this assignment may not have seemed all that radical, but in the eighties it was a different world. To the church, mere discussion of homosexuality in an attempt to show it in a positive light or to give it any sense of normalcy was seen as a way to poison the minds of children and turn them gay. For me, what was wrong was the fact that I couldn't deal with my own answers, and I certainly did not want to share my answers with my male high school teacher. The fact that he would grade me based on my responses felt like a violation of my privacy. The truth was that I was haunted by my answers which included one of my most guarded secrets. I never chose it, but felt it had chosen me. There was no way I could allow myself to be who I was, because I would lose my family, my church, and my life. I would be an outcast with nowhere to go. Though I had finally accepted that God's love for me was unconditional, that was as far as it went. I couldn't lose my family...

In typical activist and BPD extreme fashion, I made thousands of copies of this assignment and mailed them to all the residents in Gorham to show parents the type of things their kids were being required to do in high school. Calls of outrage were made to the superintendent of schools, and the school board also became involved in a review of the curriculum. My activism even caught some national attention when *The 700 Club* decided to air the handout and highlighted my efforts to get it removed from the curriculum. While I relished the positive attention I received from conservative politicians and activists, the consequences and price I ultimately ended up paying for my impulsive actions was enormous. School was no longer a safe place for me, and the teachers who had once loved and embraced me now saw me as a threat and an adversary. I left school after my junior year, and completed my diploma through home schooling.

Ami DeRienzo

Journal Entry – March 28, 1992

brother dear
my dear little brother
i was proud of you
as you took a stand today
and marched
with those you align yourself with
you didn't see me
watching so intently
you missed the tears i shed
for your well-intentioned ignorance
you missed dear old sis
standing
on the other side of the wall
with those
who are my people now
i will always be proud of you
though you fight with fury
to abolish my rights
to deny my existence
you are still
my dear little brother
and perhaps someday
you will acknowledge me as well

Author's Note: My dear brother, after going through his own journey of self-discovery and soul-searching, went on to become a champion for gay rights, and today fights with the same passion for equality as he once did for the other side.

Ami DeRienzo

CHAPTER 18

"Mom, you have to go… I'm going with you…"

She had just gotten the call that her mother was in the hospital, and it was not looking good. The cancer was starting to take over, and they didn't know how much longer it would be. While I was certainly her most challenging child, when it came to matters of the heart, at least in terms of her relationship with her own mother, it seemed I was someone she could talk to. As much as my mom and I may have battled over the years, she was in many ways still one of my best friends. My dad couldn't get the time off from work, and this was a trip I certainly didn't want her making by herself.

We made the two hour drive to Lynn where we would ultimately say goodbye to her mom. It didn't feel like this could possibly be real, not the iron lady as I would sometimes think of her. Unlike my Italian grandmother who pinched our cheeks and showered us with love and affection, this grandma was known to be a little rough around the edges. I don't recall if I ever heard the words "I love you" ever come from her lips, and she would have none of that hugs and kisses kind of stuff. She liked to be in charge of situations and was known for her ability to bark orders like a military commander. My grandfather would sit in his seat at the end of the kitchen table, a constant playful smirk on his face, while my grandmother never stopped. I don't recall her ever sitting down until it was time for her nightly beers. From early morning until the sun went down, she was a woman on a mission with things to do and people to control.

Every Christmas we would make the trek up to Grandma's house in two cars. Since Joey came along, there was just no way we could ever travel in one car again. We would walk through the narrow doorway in single file through the kitchen that was full of great aunts, uncles, neighbors, and hair dressers. If you knew my grandmother, you would also know that anyone she met along the way ultimately received an invitation to join her family at one time or another. My grandfather would mess up our already messy hair as we walked by and would greet us with a smile. My grandma would tell us to tuck in our shirts or pull up our pants, and then send us to put our coats on her bed at the end of the hall. As soon as our outerwear and the initial meet and greets were out of the way, Grandma would send us down to the basement to begin the long and arduous process of bringing up the gifts.

"Hey, whatever your name is, go down to the basement and get that bag next to the thingamajig and bring it up into the parlor."

Of course we never knew what thingamajig she was talking about, and every inch of the basement was covered with bags of presents so it was impossible to know which one was the right one. We would inevitably grab the wrong bag, repeatedly, and make numerous trips up and down the stairs. I remember the way my siblings and I used to speak in hushed tones as we tried to guess which bag to choose, as if we were on a game show where our selection of one bag would mean getting yelled at, and the other would mean we could finally get out of the dark cellar. As much as we loved my grandmother, she could sometimes be a bit intimidating, especially when you were a little kid.

What my grandmother may have lacked in bedside manner, she would attempt to make up for it at Christmas. If she had any type of interaction with you throughout the year, there was a good chance that the basement contained a present with your name on it. There was also a good chance that she bought it nine months ago and could tell you exactly how much it cost and the hell she had to go through to get it. When it came to us kids, Grandma didn't just pick up a few gifts. Each one of us, all seven of us that is, had our own trash bag full of presents. While the act of opening them up was as exciting as ever, there was bound to be the annual disappointment in finding that at least seventy-five percent of the bag contained clothes. Despite this, she never failed to get us something special that we would love and that would become a part of our childhood memories from Fisher Price toys to the latest inventions like talking machines that could do math and spelling problems. Miraculously, she always seemed to know what size clothes to buy, and had it not been for her, I doubt that any of us would have ever known what it was like to have new clothes or shoes that weren't hand me downs or from a church donation bag. The love she couldn't express in words, she expressed through gifts and by having twenty different varieties of cereal on Christmas morning so each grandchild could have their favorite.

On Christmas Eve, we would stay up late opening gifts and then find a spot somewhere in the house where we would crash. It is amazing that she found a way to make room for all of us. Thank God for large walk in closets and sleeping bags! I don't know how Grandma ever got any sleep, because in the morning we would wake to an amazing stocking full of treats that made the day as perfect as it could possibly be. Stockings were my favorite part, even when they contained the occasional stick of deodorant or toothbrush. After breakfast, the house would fill up again as aunts, uncles, first and second cousins, and distant relatives would make their way in. At some point in the day, Grandma would send my sister and me off to the *White Hen* to get her cigarettes and milk, but I think this was just an excuse to give us a little extra money so we could pick out something special for ourselves. We loved going to that store and feeling those crisp dollar bills in our hands.

As the day would go on, the kids would eventually get shooed out of the house and told to go play. With our second cousins, we would journey to the end of the road where there was a mountain of rock. At the time, this rock seemed huge, and we approached it like we were colonists about to explore the new world or a hiker tackling Mt. Everest. We felt like conquerors when we would get to the top and find the perfect spot in which to eat the snack Grandma had packed for us. Inevitably, the grumpy man that lived in the house next to the boulder would come out, threatening and chasing us away from what he felt was his rock. Seeing it as an adult that day when we drove down to say goodbye to Grandma, I was amazed at how incredibly small it had gotten when it had once seemed so big.

The machine that hovered over the bed let out a beep. Looking down at her skeletal frame and the tubes carrying oxygen, I found it difficult to believe that this could possibly be the incredibly strong superhero that I called Grandma. I immediately felt uncomfortable for her. This wasn't how it was supposed to be. It wasn't night time yet. She was the one who always took care of everyone else. This wasn't right. What troubled me most was looking into her eyes. Where there had always been a blazing fire, those eyes now looked up at me and reflected back both exhaustion and defeat. There was no fight in those eyes, only sadness and fear. As my mom and I made our way back to Grandma's house from the hospital that night, the feelings that came with seeing this mighty warrior broken were overwhelming.

We stayed for several days, visiting Grandma and doing what we could to be there for my sweet grandfather. The two of them had been married forever and as a kid sometimes I didn't understand how they could have possibly survived holy matrimony given how different they were and the enormous battles that took place between them when Grandpa felt inspired to fight back. Looking at him now, a heartbroken man who for the first time in perhaps fifty years had been handed the reigns, seeing his grief and the tender way in which he cared for her, I would never question the love that held the two of them together again.

In the years that followed, we eventually had to say goodbye to my sweet grandpa and my Italian grandmother as well. While at my grandpa's funeral, my three year old niece said, "Shh... You'll wake up great-grandpa" as she stroked his unresponsive arm. Her four year old sister understood things a little better and was able to relate losing great-grandpa to the deer they had hit with their car the night before. It was amazing the difference a year could make in a child's ability to understand and how they approached the situation with such different perspectives. At the service, the four year old started acting out and when confronted by her mom (my sister Sandy), she replied, "Mommy, I'm being bad because I'm upset! I didn't mean to kill that deer, and I didn't want great-grandpa to die. I'm sad, Mommy. I'm sad!!" This struck me as being eerily similar to my own experiences as a child, and I was grateful to see that she was able to verbalize and process it in a way that I couldn't. At the same time, her three year old sister's reality was also something I could relate to, believing that everything was okay and that there was nothing to worry about, that he's sleeping peacefully and will wake up when he's ready, because life couldn't possibly be so cruel.

While I sat there writing down what I would say at my grandpa's funeral, four year old Abby said to me, "Auntie, this isn't right. This stinks." The words of a child, so simple and yet such an accurate summary of all that I was feeling. I found myself drifting back and forth between her view and that of her three year old sister who thought loud noises would wake him up. It's just a bad dream, this isn't real, this can't be happening. I looked across the room and saw that my mother's face was not that of a fifty-five year old woman, but of a little girl, scared and broken, grieving the loss of her daddy. Later at the cemetery, my father had a look of agony and grief on his face that I hadn't seen in twenty years, since the death of his own father. He was also shedding tears that I couldn't remember having seen in the past twenty years either. This scene and its heartache was repeated again when we said goodbye to Grandma DeRienzo just a couple years later, the last of my grandparents to leave this earth.

While each of my grandparents were extremely different people, shaped by their own stories and life experiences, they all showed their love in their own ways, the best way they knew how. Reflecting back on their lives, it is overwhelming to me how much one generation impacts another and shapes who we become. While we are not our parents, our experiences ultimately come from their experiences and so on. In that regard, my grandparents will always be a part of my story, and their love and memory is something that I will always cherish.

Ami DeRienzo

Journal Entry – June 20, 1992

Sometimes I wonder if I really am crazy or if it's just that other people feel this way too but fail to express or admit it. I wish to God I could climb in another person's mind, if only for a day, and venture into the life of one of this world's normal or sane.

Life is certainly a trifling matter. In my nineteen years, I still have not figured it out though I've spent countless hours and days analyzing even the tiniest details of it. I still have yet to discover why. Why life? I mean, what is the purpose of life? Why does it continue on? Why did it begin in the first place? I find it to be quite a puzzling explanation that God was lonely and decided to create man. The infinite Creator of the universe, the one with all the answers and meanings within Himself... Why would He be lonely? If He could foresee all the pain, the bloodshed, even the murder of His own son, why did he bring it all into being? Why not live content in the clouds with the angels and sweet heavenly music? Why did He choose to go the route of heartache? I have so many questions, and so few answers that satisfy my hunger for understanding. Why, why, why??

Ami DeRienzo

CHAPTER 19

"He's back... Ami, your boyfriend's here!"

Lucy loved to tease almost as much as she enjoyed playing matchmaker. This was not the first customer she had picked out for me as a potential mate, but this time all her persistence seemed to be moving us both in the right direction. He was a good sport and would blush from embarrassment when she would interrogate him relentlessly about his intentions as she took his order. At the same time, I would be elbowing her and stepping on her toe to try to get her to stop.

It was a better time, the days of the hospital almost three years behind me. I had just finished high school and was about to start at the local Bible college, a school I had resigned myself to attending because of its affordability and small class size. For a long time I had dreams of attending a women's college in New Hampshire, but the finances weren't there. The process of applying for aid back then was overwhelming as a high school kid trying to navigate the process on my own. Instead, I decided I would work multiple jobs in order to put myself through school at the little Bible college in South Portland.

Lucy was my boss at the family restaurant where I had worked since the age of fifteen. Lucy and her husband Charlie were like surrogate parents but also a relentless big brother and sister who thoroughly enjoyed teasing us, especially when it came to matters of the heart. For many years, my older sister and I worked there together and grew to know many of the town's locals being that *The New Fourteen Main Restaurant* was the place to be. You just couldn't get two eggs, toast, home-fries, and coffee for $1.35 anywhere else that tasted so good. On a Saturday morning, it was as if every resident in the town of Gorham would come down for breakfast.

When it came to that whole dating thing, as had been the case for much of my life, I was fully programmed to accept the notion of mating with the opposite sex because that it is what you did, despite the fact that I quietly seemed to be continuously falling head over heels in love with women. Starting at a young age, I had been with several older men. My first experience had been when I was fourteen and was convinced by a twenty-one year old to skip out the back door at church one Sunday morning while my family all sat dutifully listening to that week's sermon. He took me in his car down the street to the grammar school playground and had his way with me. At the time, I had been so desperately craving affection or love of any kind that I didn't have the ability to discern between a guy's sex drive and what it meant to have someone genuinely care about you. My first sexual encounter had left me feeling empty and hollow

"Are you going to go out with him?"

Lucy never gave up. While I thought he seemed like a nice guy, it was not a case of love at first sight. He was just a customer after all, a guy who seemed like a bit of a red neck with his wads of chewing tobacco, John Deere baseball hats, and his red pickup truck with the big tires that he seemed to be infatuated with. Sometimes he was alone, and other times he came in with his buddies from the fire department and town rescue. I'd never really thought about him in that way until Lucy started to drop the hints to both of us. He was a little shy, and I certainly wasn't going to be the one to make the first move. Despite our mutual reservations, eventually we got there. We began dating, and for a while I thought that I had finally found what I'd been searching for my whole life, someone who loved me.

As I said before, there had been many men prior to James. Though I was only seventeen at the time we met, I had come to expect guys to behave in a certain way, to demand certain things, and to keep themselves at arms distance unless there was physical intimacy involved. I wasn't prepared for this, this wonderful, overwhelming feeling that perhaps someone could possibly really love me for me, that there was someone who cared more about me as a person than they did about having sex. I entered the relationship expecting him to be like all the others, but he wasn't. He was gentle and kind. He brought me roses and chocolates, gave me sweet greeting cards, and told me he loved me. He even went so far as to be the one to suggest that we wait before being intimate and that we should take it slow. Though it may not have been love at first sight, I grew to love him for the way in which he loved me or the way I believed at the time that he did. I felt myself starting to heal, starting to trust and to hope that I might someday have that normal life that others seemed to have. I thought he was different because that is what he showed me. I even believed that we would marry and have children together someday.

We had some great times together. When we weren't shooting pool at the old Pockets in Westbrook where we played Garth Brooks on the jukebox, we could usually be found 4-wheeling through the power lines trying to see how deep in the mud we could possibly get stuck. Some nights we would just go to 7-11 and grab nachos and sit listening to the police scanner. Other times we would go out in the woods and play with his guns. Despite my inability to swim and dislike of the water, he even managed to get me to go waterboarding up to his family's camp. It was a fun and freeing time when the world felt right for a while.

In another instance of irony, decades later I realized that the man in the wheelchair playing pool beside us at our old stomping ground was indeed my buddy Jake who I would meet decades later. Not only did he live near the house my grandfather built that could have been my home as a child, he also shot pool at the table beside James and I on many occasions before he ever officially came into my life. This was but another instance in which things seemed to happen as they were meant to all along.

I never quite understood what happened with James, but my utopia eventually started to crumble. While he had always enjoyed his drink, the longer we were together, the heavier the drinking became. At first it started with little things, like not calling when he said he would, not showing up when we had plans, or getting so drunk that he would pass out early in the evening. I could feel him pulling further and further away and knew that there was something going on. I'd heard rumors and had suspicions, but I still tried desperately to keep him, not wanting to give up the only romantic relationship that I had ever fully believed in. In my heart, I knew he was leaving me. I could feel it in my gut, and the more I tried to hold on to him, the more he pulled away. His eventual "It's not you, it's me" speech felt like someone was taking a straight edge razor blade and using it to slice my heart into pieces. Just when I thought I was going to be okay, I could feel myself once again spiraling out of control.

At the time that James and I separated, I was housesitting for an elderly man I had worked for since I was in junior high school. I had cared for his wife who was wheelchair bound, and they were a significant part of my life six days a week from the time I was in the seventh grade until she passed away when I was in high school. He had a house full of guns, and I just remember sitting at his kitchen table that night, drinking his alcohol and positioning that gun against my temple, wanting so badly to pull the trigger and to put an end to the pain I was feeling. I didn't think it was possible, but this sadness was even worse than what I had known in my darkest of times. To have been given hope, to have experienced love, and to have it stripped away, that was the cruelest joke life had played on me yet.

There was only one thing that caused me to put down that gun and reach for a razor blade instead, and that was love. For a man who had lost his wife of fifty years and his only daughter before that, I could not have him come home and find his adopted granddaughter's brain splattered all over his kitchen table. I couldn't do it to him, could not be the cause of any more grief. Quite honestly, I was tempted to smash the window of the truck that James loved so much, to slash those stinking tires, and to use the gun he kept in his glove compartment to end my life and would have felt no guilt at all about making him clean up the brain matter. I was not only heartbroken, but I guess I was a little bitter. Somewhere along the way, my despair had transitioned back into rage.

Obviously, I didn't go the route of ruining his truck and eventually found my way. The truth was that he really wasn't guilty of anything except for not loving me the way that I wanted him too. Although he broke my heart, leaving me was in a strange way an act of love in and of itself. Knowing he didn't love me, I know now that the most loving thing he could have done was to walk away which is what he did. I didn't quite get it back then. Instead of ending my life, I fell back into survival mode, using old coping mechanisms to fight my way through, until I could get to a better time and place.

Journal Entry – 8/12/2000

It's strange that no matter where life may take me, I always come back here to the feelings of despondency and aloneness, of desperation and pure melancholy. I feel my only comfort in life is when I crawl in bed and pull the blankets around me, but even then it can sometimes be a place of terror. My only joy is to hear my niece's sweet greeting of "Auntie," to feel loved and missed, to feel that I am special to someone, somewhere, even if it is a two year old. I feel so alone. All I want is a friend, someone to share this empty space with me. Even that seems unattainable. I try but friendship seems impossible to grasp.

I feel so hopeless because what I want and need is so very small and yet I cannot find them. I need to feel like I matter to someone. I need to have people treat me with human decency. I need human contact to break this freeze of isolation.

After all these years, after maintaining so long, is it happening again? Am I going to lose control now? Why can't I just live like others do? Why do I want to die? I don't want to die. I just don't want to live like this.

131

Ami DeRienzo

CHAPTER 20

"I know you know this, but just in case you forgot..."

My mother proceeded to read to me from a Scripture passage that referred to homosexuals as "the vilest of reprobates." I remember looking at her in that moment and speaking with a calmness that I didn't feel, suggesting that we needed some time apart and that I would move out. I was eighteen and in my first year at college when I loaded all my clothes and personal possessions into my old red Ford Mustang and drove away. What broke my heart the most was not the rejection I experienced from my parents, as that is something that I had expected would come. What really broke my heart was leaving behind my little sister and brothers who I loved more than anything in the world.

I hadn't come out to my mother, hadn't brought home a butch looking girlfriend, or ever had a discussion with her about my sexuality. What I had done was come home wearing a necklace from which hung rainbow colored rings that were a symbol within the gay community. Where my father and I now worked at the same grocery store, I imagine he had heard rumors going around about my new friendship with the gay person that worked on the checkout, but that was it. Somehow she knew, though, and given the passage she chose to read me that day, I knew she'd drawn her own conclusions. It was time to say goodbye.

It had always been there, but I guess I was too afraid or programmed to consider that it could ever be an option. I was doomed the moment the doctor had said, "It's a girl," but I had resigned myself since childhood to my inevitable fate. I could be as miserable a human being as I wanted, but it wouldn't change the fact that genetics made me a girl, and girls are supposed to like and be with boys. Though I never found much pleasure in sex, I had gotten used to the process and considered it my duty as a female. It was the emotional piece that I struggled with the most. I couldn't help but find myself incredibly restless and unengaged, wanting to connect on an emotional and intellectual level with someone, and yet finding my male companions seemed capable of only going so deep. It was also never a physical attraction where I saw a guy and thought, "Wow, he makes my heart skip a beat." It was often more about adapting to the situation which often felt like predator and prey. Of course I met a lot of good guys over the years as well, and not all my boyfriends were shallow, sex-craved monsters, but there was always something missing, even with the one I thought was the love of my life.

I was eighteen when I met her that day at work, and it was not long after James and I had broken up. I was fascinated by this woman who was nothing like what I imagined a gay person to be. Coming from a conservative, Baptist home and raised in the 70s and 80s, I was under the impression that homosexuals were people who molested children and were about as evil as it gets. There was a clear distinction between regular sinners like those who tell lies, think bad thoughts, overeat, or are envious of other's possessions, and those who commit the ultimate sin of homosexuality. In my world, I thought it ranked right up there with murderers and rapists, so the mental image of what to expect was dark.

It wasn't that my parents or anyone in the church was coming out and actually saying these horrible things, but the message was conveyed in other ways. I was taught the story from the Bible of Sodom and Gomorrah which was told in such a way as to imply that God chose to kill them all because they were gay. We never talked about what was really going on or differentiated that the city was actually condemned because instead of welcoming foreigners, they sought to gang rape them. I was also growing up in a society where calling someone a queer was clearly meant as an insult. Even in the halls of the Bible college or at church, one would hear jokes about putting all the fags on a deserted island and blowing them up. It was the way people talked back then about those they deemed to be subhuman.

My learned perception was that being gay also meant being evil, which is another reason why I never considered it to be an option. I didn't want to be that kind of person, someone who must not only be a pervert but also cruel and inhumane given the way they embraced such a sinful lifestyle. I had never met one of them before, not that I was aware of anyway, though in hindsight they were always there. Back in those days, people were good at hiding who they were for fear of people like me, something I assume probably contributed to the ignorance of people like me. It was so easy to create a boogie man out of assumptions and fears when you had no reality to compare it to. All I had was my own evil thoughts that I had run from my entire life, and prayed that God would take away for fear I might become like one of them. That was what I thought, where I was at before I met her, and then everything changed.

She was nothing like what I had imagined one of *them* might be like. She was funny and smart, gentle and kind, clearly one of the good people. She went out of her way to help, didn't smoke or even swear much, and wasn't groping anyone that I could see. She definitely did not fit my twisted idea of what a gay person would be like. I wasn't quite sure what to do with all this, but I was certainly perplexed and eager to get to know her better.

Though I had crushes on women my entire life, until I met her I had never considered that someday it might actually be more than a nagging character defect. Could I possibly be with a women and not turn into an evil monster? Could I possibly be with someone I loved and not grow horns and fangs as a result of my wickedness? I was still at the Bible college after all, surrounded by men who were studying to be preachers and women who were studying to be their wives. My brother worked on the anti-gay rights campaign the first time the idea of gays having rights came up in Portland. How could we have possibly gotten it all so wrong? This woman wasn't embarrassed or ashamed of who she was. She was in a committed, long-term relationship, and didn't care that her co-workers knew that the person picking her up from work was her partner. It was all so weird to me, but intriguing nonetheless…

As our friendship grew, I began to get excited about life in a way that I hadn't felt since those early days when I would sit in that old abandoned car in the woods with my best friend as a child and dream of being her husband.   It was as if I had finally stumbled upon the missing piece, the elusive void that had plagued me my entire life, and things suddenly made sense.   Before adolescence, back when I had no idea what sex between two consenting parties even was, it was okay for me to fall in love with my best friend. We could play house, and I could be the daddy and she could be the mommy and no one cared. I could hold her hand and think she was the most beautiful girl in the world, and love her without shame. When puberty hit and everything suddenly became about sex, it was not okay to love anymore. The same feelings that were fine before now made me a pervert. I was a sinner thinking evil thoughts, destined for condemnation and forced to choose between living a life of solitude, going to hell, or conforming to be someone I wasn't.   I was awkward and uncomfortable, not knowing how to make sense of the transitions that were taking place not in only with my body but with the new societal rules. I was taught by the world around me that who I was and what I felt was evil.

When I was a child, I thought maybe the way I could be happy and avoid going to hell or being a disappointment for the rest of my life would be if I could become a boy. I thought perhaps this would exempt me from condemnation, and that if I could just change my gender, then I would no longer have to feel guilt or shame over the thoughts and feelings that I had. When I was in my teen years and first heard of the idea of a sex change, I remember wondering if I could just commit that one "sin" (having the sex change), then maybe God would count that as a single offense that He could forgive me for and then from that point on consider my sexual attraction to women okay since it would now be "normal" as long as I was in a male body. I wondered if it would be easier on my parents to accept me as a boy once they got over the initial trauma, because sinning once is so much more acceptable than a sinful "lifestyle." I really never cared much about whether or not I could pee standing up, though it was kind of cool in theory. What I did care about was finding acceptance from my parents and from their God, and I was willing to do anything, even if it meant having to become a boy to try to make things right. What I really wanted was just to be me and for that to be okay.

While over the years my life seemed to consist of bouncing from one wild and crazy escape to another, from cutting, anorexia, substance abuse, promiscuity, and religion, to then coming to terms with the fact that I am gay.... Well, I can understand where it may all seem a bit hard to take. There may be some eyebrows raised, asking the question if perhaps these are the ramblings of an individual merely addicted to drama or seeking attention, and I understand how crazy it may sound. While going from years of turmoil to having a spiritual awakening then a year later embarking on the process of coming out may seem random, the truth is each fragment of my life led me to the next. It was all a part of a "choose your own adventure" book in which my decisions took me around the world before getting to my ultimate destination which was the discovery and acceptance of who I really am.

Ami DeRienzo

CHAPTER 21

After packing up my belongings and leaving home at the age of eighteen, the woman I had met at work and her partner opened their home to me, and I slept on their couch while searching the newspapers for apartments. When I finally found a little studio in downtown Portland across from the old *Woodford's Café*, they gave me a folding cushion that served as my only piece of furniture and was what my kitten and I ate, sat, and slept on for over a year. I grew to love the solitude of my little space. I had no television, no computer or cell phone as they hadn't been invented yet, nor did I have much of anything else, but I didn't need it. Between work, school, Melissa Etheridge, and hanging out at the café across the street, my life was full. I dropped out of Bible school after my first year, as it was clearly not a place where I felt that I belonged.

In those early years, I was amazed by the love and acceptance I found within the gay community. Until I was old enough to venture into the bars, I found friendship and support through a group called *Outright* and at the café across the street which was one of the few safe places for gay people in Maine back then. The woman who worked behind the bar at the café provided many nights of companionship and encouragement as I learned to navigate my new reality of being out on my own. She was also a bartender at *Sisters,* the women's bar that would become another surrogate home for me when I was old enough to become a patron. Over twenty-five years later, she is still a friend today, one who was a mentor during those early years and who helped me realize that there was a community ready with open arms to replace the family that I had lost.

It is strange to try and imagine what that time would have been like without the support I received from her and the rest of the gay community. When I was growing up, my family was extremely active in the church, and I always had two families, my obvious biological one and the church family who had known and cared for us throughout our lives. I was used to being surrounded by likeminded people who looked after and loved one another, who would come and visit bringing food when your mom was in the hospital having a baby, or who would greet you with a giant bear hug when you walked through the door on Sunday morning. Despite my warped perceptions of God, I grew up knowing that most of our church family was made up of kind and loving people who treated me like one of their own. The fire and brimstone existed primarily within my own head and wasn't being beaten into us when we went to church every week. It just wasn't like that. I was never a fan of the traditionalism or formalities of church, thinking it seemed superficial to get all dressed up and pretend to be someone you weren't once a week, but when it came to the people that made up the church, I knew them to be good. It was surprising to me to find this same good in the gay community, people who ultimately came to replace my church family over the years.

As I hear about gay bars all around the country shutting their doors, it creates in me both a feeling of sadness and optimism. When I was coming out over twenty years ago, there were not a lot of places you could go to feel safe, and they often consisted of one of the three local gay bars, Woodfords Café, or the pride events where there was safety in numbers. Even then, it could be frightening to walk across the parking lot or to be seen coming or going from one of these establishments, because there was always the fear that someone would be lurking in a shadow ready to try to rape or to pray the gay out of you. Things like this happened, and happened to people we knew and loved. Cars full of guys carrying baseball bats was not unheard of, and we learned quickly to be aware of our surroundings and to never walk alone. I can't imagine what life would have been like in those days without the feeling of comfort and safety the bars provided. On a social level, it was critical to have this space, because for some there was no other place to go on holidays or when you just needed to feel loved. It was not at all uncommon for gay people to be disowned by their families and treated as outcasts, especially back then.

Although the bars served alcohol, from what I could observe, the average patron was not going there to drink, at least not exclusively. They were going there to be with family, to feel loved and accepted as they were, and for a couple hours out of the day, to feel like there was a place on this earth where they belonged.

As society has evolved and people within the LGBTQ community started to find acceptance among the masses, I guess the demand for safe spaces and surrogate families has declined enough that there is no longer a pressing need for gay bars anymore. With the internet bringing people together, I suppose this also has played a role. In the same way that I am sad when I think of today's youth growing up never being able to experience life before computer technology, I also feel a twinge of sadness that many LGBTQ kids will never experience the feeling of community that we once shared at *Sisters* and the other bars. At the same time, I cannot help but feel joy in knowing that they are growing up in a world where they may not need it quite as much as we did.

For me, those years through my twenties and thirties were amazing, as I learned to experience life in a whole new way. I made wonderful friends in an environment where I finally felt like I belonged, fell in love a thousand times, and grew to embrace the world around me. Though of course there were sad times along the way, heartbreaks, and even a few villains, overall I had finally come to a place where who I was no longer haunted me, where I could live an honest life, and discover what it truly meant to feel comfortable in my own skin. While my relationship with my parents was strained for a period of time, they did not disown me, and dealt with my new life the best way they knew how. While they could never accept who I was, they learned to love me anyway which is all that I could ask.

The other night I sat in a room with a group of women who have been by my side since those early years in my coming out process. As I looked around the room, I couldn't help but reflect on what we have experienced together, from those late nights at *Becky's Diner* to group camping trips, lamenting psychotic exes to welcoming new partners into the fold, from sharing unspeakable loss and heartache to facing the harsh reality that none of us are the same people we were twenty years ago. As I took in the moment, I was hit hard with the fear that someday one of us may not be there, that as we age and life starts to throw curve balls, there may come a time when there is no one banging on those drums or strumming that guitar or playing that tambourine. When this feeling hit me, it was accompanied by a feeling of overwhelming love for these women who have become my family, people I have laughed and cried with over the years. It is hard to remember a time when they were not there. While we don't get together as often as we used to and where life has taken us in different directions, these women have been such an important part of my journey. Though my relationship with my own family became so much better over the years and I wouldn't trade them for anything in the world, this surrogate family that I found, the one who adopted me and welcomed me into their fold at a time when I was without a home, will always hold a special place in my heart.

CHAPTER 22

As much as I'd love to tell you that after coming out life suddenly became easy and drama free, that would be a lie. While my mind and my heart were certainly healthier and had found a greater peace, life still continued to happen all around me. There were times when the demons of the past would raise their ugly heads and try to pull me back. The tendency I had to gravitate toward unhealthy relationships did not end when I finally embraced my sexual orientation, nor did I suddenly become immune to heartache. Things did in many ways get better, but it was still life after all.

People came in and out of my life over the years, touching me in different ways and sharing bits and pieces of my journey. I learned how to have fun, to do crazy things like go skinny dipping on the side of the road, or take morning walks before even having my coffee and a shower. I spent a lot of time following my heart, wherever it led and whatever it told me to do, until somewhere along the line I guess I must have transitioned into adulthood and started to follow a rather routine and predictable path. I worked at the same company for almost twenty years before being laid off, entered a long term relationship of over fifteen years which I still enjoy today, became a small business owner, and at some point lost some aspects of the impulsive me that once did wild and crazy things. Of course, there are obviously some elements of my impulsiveness that have stuck around, like the crazy way in which I one day announced to my Facebook world that I was going to write this book. Overall, however, my once spontaneous nature was replaced by a rigid and reclusive person that I still don't recognize after all these years, one who goes into full panic mode at the thought of having to go to a party full of strangers or has a meltdown at the suggestion of trying something new. I need my routines, my down time, my rituals, and my comfort zones. My partner has a hard time believing that I was ever a skinny dipping kind of girl or someone who did anything that didn't involve extreme caution and analysis. I really don't know if this was a coming of age change that happened or if somewhere along the line I simply resigned myself to living in a more flat and safe world to avoid the chaos that once accompanied my passions.

Lately I have been missing the girl who had dreams of running with Laura Ingalls, and there is a part of me that would love to just sell the house, buy a camper, and go off and explore the country with my dog and my partner. That part of me would love to say the heck with this stability stuff. I'd much rather be out there pursuing my dreams and living as if there will be no tomorrow. When I start feeling this way, it always makes me think of Jake, and I hear his voice in the back of my head telling me to go for it, and to live life for today. At the same time, I know that the life that I've built is in many ways what keeps me stable. While some take medications to help keep them on track, for me the key to staying on course is often sticking to a routine and staying within my safety zones. Unfortunately, as those who take anti-depressants often complain, being healthy can sometimes mean that you feel flat, perhaps even bored, and begin to romanticize in your head about those crazy days when life was a whole bunch of things but never boring. As much as Jake always encouraged me to pursue my dreams, I know that he also would want me to be healthy. And sometimes healthy is flat...

Jake, the guy who played pool at Pockets and who was almost my neighbor, taught me so much about life in the years that I had with him. I met Jake one day when his niece discovered my online grocery store business and his family placed an order for him. I arrived at his house that day with a bouquet of flowers, ready to greet a new customer. I wasn't quite prepared for the character that awaited me in that old fashioned wheelchair. Jake took the flowers and threw them several feet so that they landed roughly on the counter, muttering that he didn't know what the hell he was going to do with those. When it came to gruff people, my initial impression of Jake was that he was one of the gruffest. I was terrified... After throwing the flowers, he went on to complain about what his sister had ordered, and expressed his displeasure with having a stranger bringing his groceries.

Though I was at first scared to go back, delivering to Jake became a regular thing, and the flowers he'd thrown were in the same exact place on the counter all shriveled up and brown when I went back a second time. Whenever I would see him, there would be something wrong with the world, someone he was mad at for something, or a customer service person who had given him some grief over the phone. For a while, I would actually dread going over for fear that he would be in a foul and angry mood, and in those early days it was sometimes stressful. I didn't know him or what to expect, and I was born with a natural aversive to gruff people.

Weeks of delivering to Jake eventually turned into years, and over the course of time, he went from being someone I feared to someone I loved. Underneath that gruff exterior was a man who had a tremendous heart, someone who had survived unimaginable challenges, heartache, and loss, and yet continued to get up every day to face the world. The more I got to know him, the more beauty I saw. What started out as a drop and run grocery delivery turned into close to an hour long visit each and every week, to the point where I would rearrange my delivery schedule just to make sure he and I would have our time together to talk about life. While our conversations generally consisted of television shows and current events, there were times when it got real, when he shared some of his journey with me or talked about the diving accident that had altered his life so many years ago. I grew to cherish that time with Jake, times when he would make me laugh with his latest brilliant ideas or his take on all that was wrong with the world. Sometimes he would just do something incredibly sweet, like the day he slipped me a $100 bill despite my protests and told me to take my partner out for dinner. Other times he would be anxiously awaiting my arrival to show off a new gadget or toy like the amazing Amazon Echo that could answer any question in the world and fascinated him like a kid first discovering an ice making machine at *Bonanza*.

After visiting with Jake weekly for approximately five years, one day I got the call from his niece that he was gone. I wasn't expecting it, wasn't prepared... I always thought I would have the chance to say goodbye, to sit by his bedside in those final hours and tell him how much he had meant to me. Over the years I had experienced and known a lot of loss, but this was different. Here was this man that once had scared me with his exterior, but had become one of my best friends. With the exception of my therapist, there was not another human being on the planet with whom I sat with for an hour every week doing nothing but looking them in the eye and talking, just because we could. I didn't realize until that first week after he was gone how significant that hour had become in my life.

One thing that Jake used to do when I would arrive was to make it a point to let me know that he had read my REALLY LONG Facebook posts that week. He would get dramatic with the hand motions and big eyes, telling me about how he had to keep hitting the "Read More" button to get to the end of it, but that despite how incredibly LONG it was, he had survived and made it through. He would then encourage me to write a book, telling me that I needed to go ahead and make it happen and that he would read it. Despite the hours we spent in conversation, Jake never knew much about my personal life or my past, certainly not what I have shared in the pages of this book. Though we muscled through that awkward talk when I had to break his heart by telling him I had a girlfriend, I'm guessing he would be a little surprised if he were here today reading this and learning about the other secrets that I kept from him. What I wouldn't give for a few more awkward conversations...

Jake's classic line was "Do have a ducky day," something he would inevitably end nearly every conversation or visit with. When I think of it, it makes me smile. For a man who had been through so much, with every day consisting of visiting nurses, bandage changes, routines, and frustrations, he still found a way to let his light shine. For those who didn't come back, perhaps all they would see was a grumpy old man sitting in a wheelchair, but for those of us who had the privilege of returning, he was an inspiration like no other. I can't help but think that Jake's survival, something that defied every odd and prediction made against him, was in and of itself an act of love. Jake was ready to go, tired of the daily battle of living while being trapped within the confines of his own body. Though he'd been in hospice multiple times, he always managed to come back to fight another day. I am convinced, however, that Jake never really fought for himself but for the many friends and family in his life that he loved. He kept going for so long, living for others when a part of him just wanted to be done. I will forever be grateful that he hung on long enough for me to have known and loved him.

At Jake's memorial, his niece shared stories about the many times throughout his life that he committed quiet acts of love, stories that touched me and that I think really exemplify the type of person he was. Like Jake himself, the stories came as a surprise to many in the room. He had a way of doing that, sneaking up on you when you weren't expecting it, and surprising you when you caught a glimpse of the man inside who looked nothing like the exterior. Jake never craved the spotlight or a pat on the back for a good deed, but did plenty of them in the shadows. One story she told was of how Jake secretly paid to have a car that was totaled in a drunk-driving accident towed to various schools to show kids the danger of driving under the influence. This is something that Jake thought to do on his own, for no reason other than the fact that he cared about kids and hated the thought of one of them getting in an accident. He never sat and talked about it, wondering if it would be a good thing for him to do; he just did it, silently without hesitation or bells and whistles. This was Jake or "just Jake" as he liked to say when people would try to call him by his birth name of Gary. Jake...the guy whose entire life was an act of love that he preferred to keep disguised within a gruff exterior.

CHAPTER 23

The car pulled up and the dogs started going wild, attacking the vehicle from both sides. Though in our normal world they would never have such freedom, this was camp and rules no longer applied when you were up here. After all, this was Monson, Maine, a place in the middle of nowhere, where people didn't get all uptight about things likes dogs being off leash. While the others went out to greet them, I was perfectly content to hang back and watch from the screen door as these strangers invaded what I felt was one of my safe spaces. I had hoped the weekend was going to be just us, my partner Katy, her sister and brother in law, and their adorable little toddler who lit up our lives and brought us so much joy. I loved our time together as a family, especially here at camp, and unlike the rest of them, I found it difficult to adapt to the changing dynamics that come with the addition of various personalities into a social situation. I didn't know these people who had pulled up although they were long-time friends of everyone else's. My anxiety was at its peak. Why did they have to come *this* weekend?

As the car door opened, angry voices carried up the driveway all the way to the doorframe where I stood. There was obviously a battle raging between the couple sitting in the car and the apprehension I was already feeling skyrocketed. I could feel myself tensing, anticipating a drama filled weekend with people I didn't know and who I had no real interest in knowing. I liked my little world the way it was, and it would be perfectly fine with me if the rest of the world continued to stay right where they were, far away from here. Unlike the kid I was in my youth who used to eagerly make new friends and embrace social contact, over the years I had become quite the recluse, content with my inner circle and determined to keep everybody else out.

The girl slammed the car door, and stormed past everyone without a word, taking off down the trail in the back of the camp that led down to the water. Her husband Frank, maintaining an air of cool and calm like only Frank can, greeted everyone as if nothing out of the ordinary was taking place as they began the process of unloading the car and getting little Chloe out of the backseat. I kept my distance, but the child quickly won me over and served as a nice distraction as she and Mackenzie greeted each other warmly. The girl eventually came back from her cooling down time, and we were introduced. In that moment, I sensed the same wary apprehension that I felt reflected back at me, and I wondered if she resented my presence too. This was the day that I met Kelly, the girl who I had no idea would eventually find a way into my heart and a place in my life, another individual who surprised me by proving that what we may reflect on the surface is not always who we are.

We survived that first weekend at camp, and as the magic of Monson often does, we eventually came together as a group and let down our guards. I suspected and later came to accept its truth that Kelly and I were alike in many ways. We did not believe in putting on a show or pretending to be someone we weren't. When she was angry, you knew it, and she didn't believe in putting on a mask simply because it was the socially acceptable thing to do. As a fellow introvert, she also needed her time and space to process emotions and to find the energy to put out in uncomfortable social situations like meeting your best friend's new girlfriend for the first time. While we were not singing *Kumbaya* by the end of the weekend, the ice had been broken and we had passed that first hurdle of going from complete strangers to acquaintances. It was a step in a long process in which we both learned to let down our guard, something that happened over the course of the next four years. It was the summer of 2002.

As time went on and it was clear that Katy's new girlfriend (that would be me) was planning to stick around for a while, we started spending more time with Kelly and Frank, taking on an auntie role with little Chloe and enjoying our time together as couples. Though it took the destruction of some walls, I grew terribly fond of them both and our love for little Chloe went without saying. There were many trips up to camp sitting around the fire or hiking in the woods, road trips through the logging trails in search of moose and other wildlife. It was our sanctuary, a place where the world stopped spinning, and there was no need for masks.

It is hard to tell this story, despite the time that has passed. What happened was wrong in so many ways, how it was her and not me. It wasn't fair, and it never should have happened. Even now, I am angry, and I am sad. She did not deserve it. It should have been me - the kid who throughout her life had toyed with death like it was a play thing. Not this amazing spirit who wanted nothing but to live her life with honesty, passion, and love, this amazing woman who would have given anything just to have more time with her little girl. They should have had more time. She should have gotten to see her beautiful child go off on her first date or to walk down that aisle at graduation. She should be here now, laughing with us as we comb through the old home videos of her and Frank being goofy at Thanksgiving or telling Chloe stories about her wild and crazy days. It should have been me, not her... And yet this was one more instance in which God was silent, denying me the right to take her place.

Over the years I grew to know and love Kelly in a way that my heart never anticipated after that first day at camp when I had pegged her so wrong. She was a gentle spirit, an artist who was passionate about her convictions and who was content to live life simply, someone who cared about justice and truth and seemed to experience pleasure in eating kale, perhaps the only thing about her that I never fully grew to appreciate. She found such joy in being a mom and despite the occasional lover quarrels, adored her husband Frank, someone who would go to the ends of the earth for her and her for him. They were a beautiful family who stole our hearts, hearts that were broken with unimaginable grief when that day came.

Grief is a funny thing. Sometimes you experience grief before you've even encountered the loss because the mere thought of losing someone you love chokes you in a way that feels like your entire spirit is being starved of oxygen. Then there is that other kind of grief in which there is no way you could have possibly imagined how it would be, when you thought you were somewhat prepared only to find that there is nothing in the world that could have prepared you for this. While you might be able to find a way to manage your own grief, perhaps you never anticipated the added horror of what it would be like to have that grief compounded by seeing the grief that others in your life are also experiencing, like when you look across the room and realize that the empty, sick to your stomach feeling that you are experiencing doesn't even come to close to the agony of your dear friend's spouse, child, brother, or parent. And then you grieve even more, not only for yourself, but for them, realizing that the suffering has only just begun.

There is no way to find the appropriate words to describe what happened. I can't even attempt to shroud it in something that sounds literary. It sucked, pure and simple. There was no reason or justification for it. And although I believe things happen in life for a reason and eventually, someday, supposedly it will all make sense and that good can come out of bad, I still don't anticipate ever accepting that what happened was "for the best" as people trying to make sense of horrible things are known to imply. It was a horrific, miserable, awful thing that made no sense then or now. Kelly was diagnosed with Ewing's Sarcoma, an extremely rare form of cancer, so rare that the odds of someone getting it are about one in a million, and yet it chose her. As rare as it is, it is even rarer in adults and more common in males than females, so those odds of one in a million were even more unlikely. Even statistically it was wrong.

The years following the diagnosis in some ways are a blur. There were moments of hope followed by soul crushing disappointments, but throughout it all, Kelly was determined to fight and to stay strong. Wanting to be there for her family, she was not ready to give up or even consider it as an option. She tried various treatments and holistic alternatives, miracle potions that promised results and radical diets aimed at starving the cancer cells. She was an extremely independent soul who was used to taking care of herself, and I think perhaps one of the hardest parts of her journey was when the cancer robbed her of her mobility, forcing her into a wheelchair. Through it all, though, she got up every day determined to fight like hell, and never uttering a word of complaint or self-pity.

I remember one day little Chloe decided she wanted to push her mom around in her chair outside, but was determined to do so at high rates of speed without the safety of a seat belt or harness. After witnessing a moment of the action, I was quick to call out to her that it wasn't a good idea, that she could hurt her mom if she didn't slow down. Kelly looked up at me, in her soft and gentle way with a playful spark in her eye and a smile on her face, and said, "It's okay... We're just having fun. She can push me." And off they went. In my head all I could envision was the chair hitting a pothole and Kelly's frail body going airborne. Of course she knew the dangers, too, and yet it was more important to her to be able to hear Chloe giggle and to see her little girl's face light up with joy as they flew down the street at full speed than to worry about something so trivial as a broken bone.

At this time in my life, I was working as a night manager at the grocery store in Scarborough which was within ten minutes of Kelly's home in South Portland. While her daughter was at school and the rest of the world was working a traditional 9-5 job, my late night shifts allowed me the blessing and the opportunity to spend many of my days with my new friend. Despite the years of getting to know each other, we were still both introverts and our time together was generally not filled with frivolous conversation or chattiness. In fact, there was actually a lot of silence, something that we both became comfortable with over time. When Kelly got to a point where we did not feel safe leaving her home alone, I was there more regularly, spending my days with her, hanging out, maybe doing some laundry or light stuff around the house to entertain myself while she napped. It was an honor to be there, even though I knew we would never have the type of history together or the kind of relationship that she seemed to have with her other friends. My only regret was that I didn't embrace her sooner, like the moment she drove up that driveway and slammed that silly door. I was running out of time, and now this beautiful human being was slipping away from me. I wished I had tried harder, had opened myself up and let down my guard so we could have had a little more time.

That horrible day will forever be engrained upon my memory. She was only thirty-five... My partner Katy had gone to spend the night with her, and I got a call that morning to tell me that she was gone. We knew it was coming, and that it would be soon, but it still felt like a kick to the stomach, the kind that produces vomit in the back of your throat. I was not prepared to see the grief of an eight year old child or the father who rocked her in his arms trying desperately to provide some level of comfort. I was not prepared for the floodgates of grief her family endured or watching my own partner's heart break as she said goodbye to her childhood friend. We were all broken. I remember that day at Kelly's house, blasting Sinead O'Conner and screaming until we could scream no more, as if we were tribal creatures without the ability to verbalize the depth from which the emotions came. All I could think was that it should have been me... What I wouldn't have given for God to have allowed me to take her place. It was no longer because I wanted to die, but because I wanted so desperately for her to live.

CHAPTER 24

Last night my partner of over fifteen years and I went to the theater to see the movie *The Shack*. I found it interesting that we went to see this particular movie at this particular moment in time when I just happened to be at this stage of my story. We almost never go the movies or venture out anywhere after dark anymore, but for some reason, last night we went out on a whim, and I found myself sitting in the movie theater weeping for almost two hours as so much of my own journey of healing, forgiveness, and reestablishing critical relationships flashed before me on the big screen. It also brought back a great deal of grief and all the hurt and anger that came with it. Though it has been over ten years since we lost Kelly, and over thirty years since my grandfather's death, the feelings of abandonment and questioning of God that came with these and other experiences still stung.

In many ways, this movie felt like my own story and the story of countless others that I have known, bringing back the emotions from childhood of the disappointment that came when things too complex for us to ever understand invaded our world and robbed us of our innocence. I had trusted God with a child-like faith, only to feel like He had let me down and that I would never be good enough. In my mind, He punished me by taking away so many things that I loved over the years. I felt that I had been abandoned when I had needed Him most. There were years of wounds that I did not share in these pages - anger, sadness, and grief that I was carrying and felt that I was carrying alone. I thought of God as this sadistic being in the sky who toyed with us, creating us to be something and then condemning us for being the person He created us to be in the first place. I felt like I was a failure and would always be a disappointment, "a sinner in the hands of an angry God" as the old theologian Jonathan Edwards once wrote.

When I was a toddler, I remember my mom would play this record that talked about the return of Christ that would cause me to cry and beg her to turn it off every time she would play it. Being a toddler, I obviously wasn't having conflicts of sexual orientation at the time, but I was terrified of the God on that record, thinking He was angry and was coming for me. Of course my parents were not crazy radicals who taught their kids that God was some scary monster. We were taught that "God is Love" in Sunday school, but there were other things that were naturally inferred that I suppose gave me such a warped view of who God might be.

I was the type of kid who couldn't in good conscience step on an ant house and who worried when washing my hair that I might be hurting the shampoo by squishing it around too much. Being told that God allowed His own son to be nailed on a cross and left to die or that He'd ordered the angels to kill every first born child in the city... Listening to the story of Noah's ark and how God killed everybody because He thought they were bad or how he ordered Abraham to kill his own son... All the "God is Love" posters in the world couldn't convince me that a God who would do such things could be one of the good guys. Combine this with the common threats parents make to their children about how God is watching them and being told that thinking a bad thought is just the same as actually doing it, and it doesn't take much to distort a message in the mind of an overly sensitive, literal, and analytical kid. It especially doesn't take a whole lot when you throw in a dead grandpa who you apparently killed with your bad thoughts.

The movie we saw that night touched my heart because when I was a little girl, I prayed to my "Papa" as God is referred to in the movie, trusting He would take care of me. I believed that if He was a loving God that He would most certainly save an innocent bird or bring back my grandpa. I'd been told that faith could "move a mountain," and I believed it, being the literal kid that I was. From all the stories I'd heard, I thought God was the real deal and was fully expecting miracles that never came. I became disillusioned at a young age and thought somehow that His inaction was a direct result of my not being good enough.

While the stories that I've shared may seem disconnected or even all over the place, they are all intertwined. The things I experienced in childhood brought me to that place of despair and searching in my preadolescence and teen years as I dealt with my shame and feelings of inadequacy. That night when I became overwhelmed at the thought that God might not be who I thought He was, and finally came to accept that His love for me was real, something changed. From that day on, I knew that no matter who I was, where I went, or what I did, that there wasn't an angry man in the sky looking to zap me, but instead a father figure who was there ready to love, to forgive, and to accept me for who I am, as I am. It was like having spent your entire life trying to win the approval or acceptance of a distant parent and finally hearing those simple words, "I'm proud of you, kid." It was like sitting there in literature class in seventh grade and having someone tell you that you had done well and believing that they meant it. It wasn't like I was suddenly disillusioned into thinking that I was a perfect human being or feeling like I'd been given a free pass to do whatever I wanted, but it was about accepting my humanness and the feeling that the heavy chains that I was carrying around were finally gone. I did not need to punish myself anymore, didn't need to hide my head in shame or run from a God who knew everything about me but loved me anyway.

What doesn't make a lot of sense to some people who I know is how could I possibly go from being a Bible school student who was doing public speaking at religious events to suddenly being a lesbian hanging out in gay bars? How could I possibly reconcile my lifestyle and claim to believe in God when there are passages in Scripture that they believe say that who I am is an abomination of the worst kind? Then there are others who are equally dumbfounded, wondering how I can possibly believe in a God that to them represents nothing more than an excuse to promote hatred and discrimination, bigotry and fear. They see being gay and believing in God to be as contradictory as people in the church might but for much different reasons. And once again, I find myself with that old junior high school dilemma, where I am stuck in the middle in a world where I don't really fit in, but that is okay. It took many years of going to "the shack" for me to fully reconcile these things myself, and it would likely take another whole book to share that journey with you. Regardless, my intent is not to promote some theological ideology or push my beliefs upon anyone. This was simply my journey and how I found hope in a world that at times felt hopeless.

I hated myself intensely for so long. I wanted to kill the monster inside me, the girl who thought evil thoughts, and the one who was destined for hell. Then one night I came to accept the fact that I was loved just the way I am, imperfections and all, no strings attached, no payment required beyond what had already been paid. From that moment, my life changed because I finally accepted that God's love was like that of a parent, the type of parent who loves without condition... For the first time in my life, I felt free to be who I was and know that it would be okay, that I still had a Papa who saw me through an entirely different lens than the one the world or the church judged me through. I was not His failure or some cruel joke He decided to play. I was His child, loved unconditionally the way I am.

The reason why I share this part of my journey is for those of you who may be experiencing your own spiritual conflicts, perhaps similar to mine. Maybe you too have spent your life feeling like you were never going to be good enough. Maybe you were taught, whether intentionally or unintentionally, that there was an angry God up there in the sky ready to zap you and perhaps you have never known the freedom of letting that go. Maybe you too have wrestled with issues of gender confusion or sexual orientation and thought there was no way God could ever love you because you grew up in a world where you were taught that you are somehow less than human. Maybe you were a little kid with your own dead grandpa or baby bird, something that broke your heart or caused you to lose your faith in someone greater than yourself. Wherever you are, whoever you are, whatever the source of your pain, if sharing these little bits and pieces of my life does anything, I hope that it conveys to you that you are not alone, that there is hope, and that there is love all around you even when you can't see it.

One thing that I have learned over the years is that we don't always recognize love. Sometimes love on the surface can appear brutal and stomach churning, looking like anything but what we think love should look like. Maybe it is a parent who makes us so angry that we want to scream, a God who sends His own Son to die a painful and horrible death, or a kid who picks up a razor blade instead of a gun. Sometimes acts of love are subtle. Maybe it's that person in your life pretending that they don't want that last spoonful of pasta, a bag full of presents sitting in a dark corner in the basement, or a locked cabinet full of snacks. Maybe it's that teacher who cares enough to draw a smiley face, the bartender who listens with a sympathetic ear, or the neighbor who keeps on hand a fresh supply of bananas. Whether you believe in God and have a moment of spiritual epiphany or simply experience that feeling of awe by making eye contact up close and personal with a moose, there is love surrounding you, and it is worth hanging on until you discover exactly where it may be hiding. Perhaps you are someone like Jake and maybe you are tired and find that it is hard to keep going day after day, but there is someone out there like me waiting to meet you in the future, someone whose life you are meant to touch and to change, and it is for this reason that you must go on.

The best advice I ever received in my life came from a fellow patient in the psychiatric ward. We were sitting on top of a dumpster in the parking lot of the hospital smoking a cigarette, just coming back from a group outing. My friend looked at me and said the simplest thing. She said, "You've got to fake it, until you make it." Those words have stuck with me all these years, and I believe they are the key to survival for many people like me. Sometimes it really is just a matter of hanging on and going through the motions whether you feel like it or not, knowing that eventually someday things will get better, and you will find your way. As someone who has been in that darkness and knows how hard it can be to hold on or to fake it when you want to curl up and die, I do not say these words lightly. I know it sounds contrite and overly simplistic. And I know how hard it is to function and to face another day when you have lost hope. But if nothing else, please remember this... You are good enough. You are worthy. And you are loved. Just the way you are...

Life may not make much sense right now, but I promise you that it does eventually get better. It will never be free of pain, but there will come a day when you are able to look back and be thankful that you went through the motions and got through this day when you experience your future joy. There is love all around you. Even if you aren't able to see it or feel in this moment in time, it is still there, waiting to take you in its arms and show you the many wonderful things that lie ahead. Everything in life, even the horrible things that don't make any sense, are a piece of the puzzle. Some pieces are harsh and ugly, but are still a critical part of the bigger picture, one that someday you will hang on your wall and see in its entirety, and I hope that when you do, it makes you smile...

AFTERWARD

There are many more stories I wish I could tell you, and people who came into my life over the years deserving of a space in these pages. I think of the girl introduced me to crescent rolls and taught me how to have my first healthy and loving relationship, the individual who affectionately called me "Renzo," or the girl who battled addiction that I spent months living with in a 70's style lilac camper complete with Grateful Dead decals and all. I didn't tell you about what it was like to be an adult who found herself in an abusive relationship, or the second or third time that I landed in a psychiatric ward for depression in my late teens and early twenties.

I never got around to bragging about my beautiful nieces and nephews and how much joy they have brought into my life, how proud I am of the beautiful human beings my siblings grew up to become, or how my parents morphed into Super Grandma and Grandpa overnight. I didn't tell you how close we all have become, the way in which I adore each and every one of them, and how blessed I am to have such a wonderful family.

These pages were devoid of much that has transpired in the past twenty years, including my life with my partner who is an honest, decent, wonderful human being who gives of herself every day not only to me but to everyone around her. I didn't share the many challenges and losses that we have experienced together, how completely opposite we are in just about every way, and how we have grown over the years.

I didn't tell you about how I picked myself up and went on after thinking my world had ended when I was laid off from my job, or how I started a business that I love where I have met many wonderful people like Jake. There are so many stories, and while this book may contain a great deal of sadness, for every bit of heartache, there have been equal amounts of good, acts of love and kindness that present themselves all around me each and every day and touch my life.

While I could have filled a book taking you through a single vice, a loss, or a heartbreak, instead I chose to provide you with a snapshot of isolated incidents that were separate and yet intertwined. While some feel that sharing intimate details of your life is difficult, for me it is easy because much of what I have shared is so far removed from who I am today that it no longer feels personal. I am no longer the kid with borderline personality disorder cutting my wrists in the bathroom or being treated for mental illness. I am not the girl driving around in a pickup truck shooting rifles and plowing through the mud in 4-wheel drive. I'm not the speaker on the stage talking to hundreds of kids about my experiences. I am just a regular forty-something year old whose pant size has been growing far too quickly and who on some days seems to have lost all motivation for human contact. I'm the person who would rather poke out their eyeball with a sharp instrument than talk to someone on the phone, and who sometimes goes into full panic mode at the mere suggestion of getting together for anything social. I'm the auntie who likes to spoil the little ones and the spouse who gets in an argument on a regular basis about really stupid things. Yes, my crazy may sometimes look a little different than others, but in the end I am not the person I was and not who I will be.

There are days when I still dream of running through the fields with Laura Ingalls, of climbing into Pa's lap and having him explain the complexities of life and sneaking one of those sugar cubes. Other days I just resign myself to the fact that life is slowly passing me by and that there is much work left to be done before I find that one day my time has come. Whatever happens, whether I have another forty years on this planet or forty days, it is finally okay and I am at peace, grateful for every wonderful person that has come into my life and been a part of this journey.

Please Don't Go It Alone...

If you or someone you love is hurting, there are people who care and who are able to help. If you are a student, please reach out to your school guidance counselor, nurse, parent, teacher, doctor, minister, or other adult figure that you trust.

There are also people available at the National Suicide Prevention Lifeline 24 hours a day:

1-800-273-8255

While I am not a professional and cannot offer any type of counseling, if something in this book touched you and you would like to reach out to me directly, I would love to hear from you.

Please feel free to send me an email at amiderienzo@gmail.com.

Ami DeRienzo

ABOUT THE AUTHOR

Ami DeRienzo is a native Mainer who currently lives in Scarborough, Maine with her partner Katy and their fur baby Darlan, a border-collie lab mix rescued from Alabama. She is the proud auntie of too many nieces and nephews to count, and is also a small business owner. *Acts of Love* is Ami's first publication, though she dreams of someday pursuing her love for writing on a full-time basis.

Made in the USA
Columbia, SC
17 March 2022

57780615R00091